THE BIBLICAL LINK TO ADDICTIONS

Colin Garnett BA Th.

authorHOUSE®

AuthorHouse™ UK Ltd.
500 Avebury Boulevard
Central Milton Keynes, MK9 2BE
www.authorhouse.co.uk
Phone: 08001974150

First published by AuthorHouse   05/06/2011

ISBN: 978-1-4567-7324-3

CONTENTS

INTRODUCTION
The Biblical Link to Addiction & Recovery

With hindsight I believe it is the result of a personal subliminal search, which grew into a progressive analysis, which then eventually led to the alignment of the conditions set forth in this book. I, the author, now believe these conditions to be the innate roots, inevitable fruits and intrinsic requirements for recovery from addictive disorders. Whilst the journey we are about to take will chronologically demonstrate how individuals from any sphere of society could fall prey to the deceptively slippery slopes which lead deep into the valley of addiction, we will not leave you there. I am a survivor of that valley and have in recent years witnessed hundreds of struggling men and women find their way out of addictions grip and into recovery through the insights set forth in this book. This spiritual journal will not only illuminate the root causes of addiction; it will go on to guide addiction's various conditions to the pathway out of the darkness.

This book will also illustrate how the Church must seek to understand the varied 'therapeutic needs' of the lost and the dying before they can claim any rite of passage to 'make disciples' of them. Similarly, this book will call 12 steppers and the secular therapeutic world to give an account of its contempt for the attempts of Christianity in its endeavors of influencing the drug world. The spiritual and psychological conditions which constitute the thesis for the Biblical Link to Addiction and Recovery are as follows, set out in their chronological order of progression:

DECEPTION

EXPERIMENTATION

RECREATION

ESCALATION

ADDICTION

DETERMINATION

DESPARATION

INTERVENTION

DEVASTATION

LIBERATION

CONFESSION

ILLUMINATION

DEPRESSION

REFLECTION

SUBMISSION

DEFLECTION

Theories offered in this book stem from insights gathered over a 30-year period of the following personal experience:

Eighteen months of experimental and recreational chemical use as a teenager. Eighteen months of increasing chemical abuse with a decrease in morals and values. Fifteen years of intravenous heroin addiction, including six years in prisons and rehabs. Eighteen months intermittent therapy in Europe's top addiction treatment clinics. Five years of daily involvement and personal application of the 12-Step programme. Four years of Theological study to BA Degree level. Therapeutic training in Europe's top addiction treatment clinics for Addiction Counseling. Employment in Addictions Counseling in the world's top addiction treatment clinics. Development of three extremely effective addiction treatment facilities.

CHAPTER ONE

ALCOHOLISM NEEDS THEOLOGY LIKE CHRISTIANITY NEEDS THERAPY

In reflection over the combination of experiences allotted to my life, and as the sands of time pass by at a seemingly increasing pace, my motivation for writing The Biblical Link to Addiction and Recovery is further enhanced, even to a point of urgency, by the thought of how much of a shame it to die with this amount of proven life changing information. If the information in this book is not from God, then what I am documenting will at least serve as a guide into the spiritual essence within the killer dynamics of addictions and as an interesting academic exercise. However, I am of the firm conviction that the explanations within each window of experience will offer answers to questions yet discovered within the hearts and minds of some very confused addicts and their families, particularly from within my central window of 12-Step Recovery membership.

Whilst proving, on the one hand, to be my most emotionally and psychologically developmental period, my season within the 12 Step recovery community simultaneously created within me a growing belief that spiritually, their 'disease' ethos was slowly and insidiously becoming my gravest threat. The emotional and psychological development came from the open forum for exposing character flaws, insecurities and behaviours on a daily basis which were, on the whole, received with unconditional positive regard. The cancerous threat came from having to resign myself to a life of seeking affirmation from 'the group' and the corporate 'encouragement' to 'create a god of my own understanding' from which I could then source daily strength for recovery. Thereafter, abstinence from the life-controlling chemicals was the only requirement for certification of authenticity.

1

Colin Garnett BA Th.

This book exposes a wide variety of spiritual and psychological pot-holes and blind-spots which constitute an addiction. Therefore, required dynamics for recovery must be established upon theological foundations and therapeutic fillings. Let us return to the valley of addiction and place an hash (#) next to theological principles and underline the therapeutic dynamics for the counseling context, from the 16 dynamics of the valley ...

DECEPTION #	**LIBERATION #**
<u>**EXPERIMENTATION**</u>	**CONFESSION #**
<u>**RECREATION**</u>	**ILLUMINATION #**
<u>**ESCALATION**</u>	**DEPRESSION #**
<u>**ADDICTION**</u>	**REFLECTION #**
DETERMINATION #	**SUBMISSION #**
DESPARATION #	<u>**DEFLECTION**</u>
INTERVENTION #	
DEVASTATION #	

We immediately see that approximately 25% of the problems are of a therapeutic nature. Therefore the danger is that even if we assume the best of Christian ministers to be fully conversant with counseling people through the theological themes highlighted, their best theology is still going to leave people wanting.

On the other hand from a secular stance, it could be argued, the most clinically qualified therapist making numerous inroads into the worldview of addicts by addressing the therapeutic topics, may completely miss the mark when it comes to the need of scratching addicts where they itch spiritually. Therefore it would appear that both the Christian and the secular world of addiction counseling have some of what the other needs.

Articles abound on the 'evils' of the 12-step recovery programme and not just from Christian world. One 'junior member' of the Australian

Atheist Federation is recently quoted on their website as saying: "I would say that 12 step programs meets the definition of a cult in some ways - they have a teaching that is outside the mainstream, there are dire consequences for separating yourself from the group and there are enigmatic founders".

In their defense however, in the A. A. 'Big Book' they make the following statement as an introduction to the12-Steps: 'With all the earnestness at our command, we beg of you to be fearless and thorough from the very start. Some of us have tried to hold on to our old ideas and the result was nil until we let go absolutely. Remember that we deal with alcohol; cunning, baffling, powerful! Without help it is too much for us. But there is one who has all power; that one is God. May you find Him now! Half measures availed us nothing. We stood at the turning point. We asked His protection and care with complete abandon'.

The Twelve Steps are as follows:

1. We admitted we were powerless over alcohol and that our lives had become unmanageable.

2. Came to believe that a Power greater than ourselves could restore us to sanity.

3. Made a decision to turn our will and our lives over to the care of *God as we understood Him.*

4. Made a searching and fearless moral inventory of ourselves.

5. Admitted to God, to ourselves, and to another human being the exact nature of our wrongs.

6. Were entirely ready to have God remove all these defects of character.

7. Humbly asked Him to remove our shortcomings.

8. Made a list of all persons we had harmed, and became willing to make amends to them all.

9. Made direct amends to such people wherever possible, except when to do so would injure them or others.

10. Continued to take personal inventory and when we were wrong promptly admitted it.

11. Sought through prayer and meditation to improve our conscious contact with *God as we understood Him*, praying only for knowledge of His will for us and the power to carry that out.

12. Having had a spiritual awakening as the result of these steps, we tried to carry this message to alcoholics, and to practice these principles in all our affairs.

The Biblical Link to Addictions and Recovery wants to align itself with all arguments and suggest: 'let's meet in the middle; people are dying within earshot of our bickering'.

Yes, there are dangers within the doctrine of the 12 step programme, but it is no more dangerous than some of the stuff being preached in a pulpit near you each Sunday. Yes, some of the founders of the 12 step recovery programme got up to some weird stuff, but again, it's no weirder than some of the behaviours being found in some Churches these days.

An alcoholic lady in our care recently told me; 'at first, my higher power was my daughter and then it became the AA group, and then, sometime after I had exposed all my shameful deeds, I fell in love with God in and through The Lord Jesus Christ. Without her AA programme, it could be argued that this girl may never have come to Christ.

If we undertake the journey through the valley of addiction, we can reconcile theology and therapy and establish boundaries between the two by illustrating the why, where and when theology and therapy must harmonize and integrate the principles of the step programme.

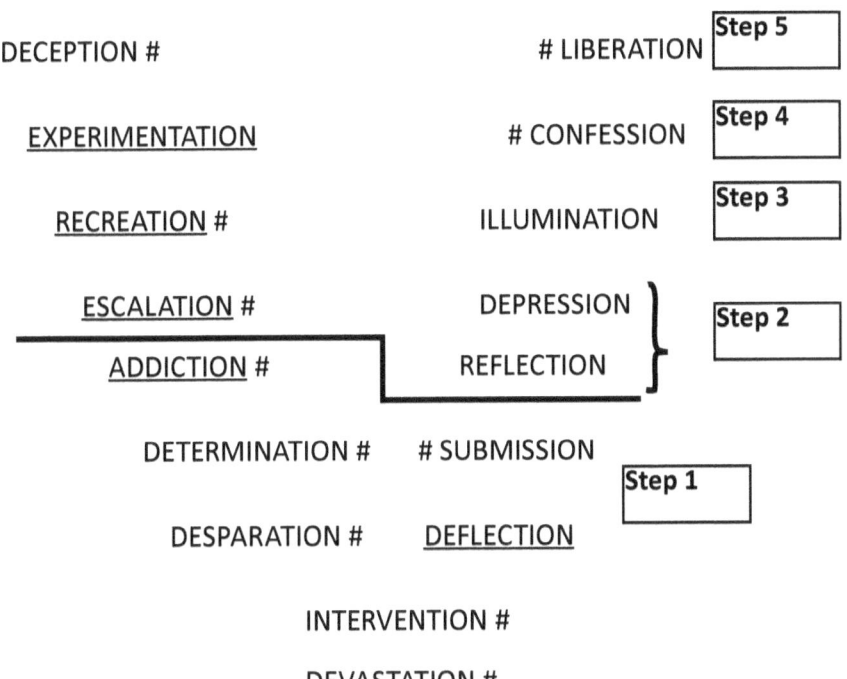

DECEPTION #

EXPERIMENTATION

RECREATION #

ESCALATION #

ADDICTION #

DETERMINATION #

DESPARATION #

INTERVENTION #

DEVASTATION #

LIBERATION — Step 5

CONFESSION — Step 4

ILLUMINATION — Step 3

DEPRESSION

REFLECTION — Step 2

SUBMISSION

DEFLECTION — Step 1

Enjoy the journey.

CHAPTER TWO

LOCATION AND CONDITION IDENTIFICATION

Following my conversion to Christ in prison in 1993, I slowly started to see how my recovery efforts up until that point had actually been built on sand, waiting to collapse. In truth, whilst to many I had become a role-model 12-stepper, I had also become a 'serial relapser'. In Christ, I knew, now, relapse is simply not an option. On release from prison I soon became a member of a local Church and in a dangerously naïve state, expected the same degree of self-disclosure in Church and quickly set out confessing my intimate personal struggles from within my heart and within my imagination. Elders and laymen alike, however, shrank back from my 12-step way of 'exposing the exact nature of my wrongs' (Step 5) and I soon slowly began to feel alone in 'my naive quest for cleansing'. Not only so, I slowly started to find myself becoming the 'project' of various 'ministers', many of whom regularly cast a variety of demons out of me.

During one prayer session one of these Elders saw me clicking the end of my thumb nail against the tip of my index finger nail. This was something my mum used to do when I was a little boy, she would pretend that there was a tiny bird in my ear. I was really enjoying this memory when the Elder spoke out saying it was a physical manifestation of a 'demon of masturbation'. In the beginning of these 'manifestations' I decided to play along, only to find his critter being cast out of me several times. Each time I played along, though, I would be left feeling second class, let down, patronized and even used in some distorted way. Because my struggle had been described as something 'demonic' I slowly started to feel like an inferior Christian. When the problem continued I could only conclude that 'it' had taken up permanent residency and that night I lay in bed and considered the possibility that I might be a false Christian. This decay was enhanced when I started to pick up on how no one else in Church ever gave voice to the same or any similar type of struggle. I slowly started to doubt my beliefs and then I started to believe my doubts – right started to sound wrong and wrong started to sound right. It was then that I looked back to my miraculous conversion and the wonderful love and light and peace that my relationship with God had given me and I knew: what He has done cannot in me be faked. My doubts were rooted in and fuelled by me actively playing the game of Christianity and not speaking out. Several years earlier I had damaged my back in a prison gym. I can pin point the incident because of the intensity of the injury. It was still bothering me at that time and I decided to test the healing powers within my Elders once and for all and I went to them for prayer. After the laying on of hands one of them spoke out: "The Lord has just told me that you were born with one leg longer than the other and this is the cause of the pain". They sat me down and one of them held both my feet on his lap and examined my legs. He then confirmed that he could see the deformity and he burst into praying for me. He then declared that he had seen the leg grow and that The Lord has just healed me. It was at that moment that I grew, not in stature, but in resolve, because I just knew, this guy is pulling everyone's leg.

In hindsight, I now know that most of my masturbation was an unpreventable fruit of a compressed emotional and psychological state of confusion and neediness. I was actually self-medicating in a sense, to release my frustration whilst simultaneously self-comforting due to unmet needs for intimacy with a female. Spiritually I started to grow disillusioned. Not only was I starting to see 'leaders' creating a ministry for themselves around me; it was exactly what some

of the 12-Step Recovery Community members had tried to warn me about and I felt trapped between the two. I had within me a burning desire to share the truth of Jesus in the recovery community, yet a niggling fear of introducing any of them into a situation where they might subsequently relapse, because I know within my heart, if I had not experienced the deeply profound encounter that I had had in prison and the subsequent freedom in Christ, I do not believe I would have remained in Church or in recovery.

At the writing of this book therefore, my concluding convictions are:

1. A sub-culture of addiction seduces more naïve teenagers to its deadly deceptive regime than the Church does to what in truth should be a more attractive and constructively honest alternative.

2. A mid-culture of 'self-help' appears to offer the 'diseased' addict a more attractive alternative than the misery of active addiction and/or the prospect of joining a Church.

3. A genuine spiritual awakening toward the God of the Bible from within the dark ranks of the addiction culture would not only expose many ministers as inadequate; it would expose many vulnerable members of many congregations to various forms of abuse.

The Biblical Link to Addictions and Recovery addresses struggling members of addiction and/or those in early stages of the 12-step recovery culture, and Christian ministers unsure of how to welcome and nurture those who profess to have been converted. It takes the hand of each, drawing each towards the other, offering an understandable middle ground on a Theological foundation.

In 1772 reflecting on his conversion to Christianity, John Newton wrote: "Amazing Grace, how sweet the sound, that saved a wretch like me, I once was lost, but now am found, was blind, but now I see". Not only have Mr. Newton's words stood the test of time, they are still trumpeting the celebration of salvation from within the hearts of every Born Again Christian known to God. However, it also stands steadfast in a sad and all too often ignored irony, how people lost and blind to the possibility of an intimate loving relationship with God, can and often do heartily sing these same words with passion and sincerity. During personal therapy for my own chronic heroin addiction, I tearfully sang several passionate renditions of Mr. Wesley's anthem in a duet with a dying alcoholic. Days later, I rejoined the dark ranks of the drug culture and was once again breaking into houses, buying heroin and injecting myself into oblivion.

Whilst the song had had a therapeutically satiating effect within me as I sang, only now do I believe this to be because it gave recognition and expression to my inner most needs for direction, illumination and liberation. The difference between Mr. Newton and me was subtle but deadly;

- I found it liberating to sing

- Mr. Newton sang because he was free

Had someone spoken into Mr. Newton's life before he wrote Amazing Grace with the question; 'what are your key developmental needs? I think the response would have probably sounded something like:

1. I need to know exactly what my condition is

2. I need to know exactly what the solution is

3. I need to know exactly what my motivation is

Now take a dying intravenous heroin addict from anywhere in the world, pull him out of his box by his ankles and ask the same question; I believe you will find the response would be exactly the same.

People are neither lost needing to be found, nor are they blind needing sight *because* of their addictions; they turn to chemicals *because* they are lost and blind.

The following hypothesis therefore stands in contradiction of the contemporary approach to addiction treatment offered by many clinics worldwide, in that it traces and highlights a Biblical root for the depravity of man's heart and the need for a miracle, as opposed to the disease concept and its self-help/damage control approach.

CHAPTER THREE

THE ROOT DEBATE – DECEPTION

The World Health Organization's approach in treating addiction as a disease originally stems from the following conclusions:

1. It responds to treatment

2. It gets progressively worse if ignored

3. It eventually kills

I recently imagined myself as a desperate parent whose daughter was seemingly dying right in front of me. I imagined what it must be like to be afraid of my child and to regularly have to experience the erratic emotional outbursts that now characterized our once loving relationship.

I forced myself into the shoes of a dad whose girl was skin and bone with smouldering rage, because all too often in addiction treatment circles parents can be heard: "But I just don't understand". Family members stare into their own abyss of hopelessness as loved ones appear to turn evil and slowly die before their eyes. Various doctors come up with various medications which appear to offer temporary chemical solutions in their sincere attempts to at least offer the desperate families a degree of control. However, in reality, parents continue to witness the true image of their child growing increasingly darker under a continued destructive influence of an addiction. Months and years of destruction reduce many families to settling for a 'happy-medium' for their loved ones of a satiated effect of prescribed mood stabilizers and/or anti-depressants.

Hopelessness increases as the destruction progresses. In the darkness of late nights and the twilight of early mornings, young addicts lie awake in one room, overwhelmed by a burning pre-occupation of where the next hit is coming from, whilst parents lie awake in the next room, overwhelmed with confusion, uncertainty and fear.

The deepest need of everyone concerned is an empowering explanation of exactly what is taking place, which simultaneously illuminates and steers towards hope and peace of mind. Illumination needs to take place within the often distorted perceptions of addicts, families and professionals about the spiritual Link to Addictions. Because we struggle to understand the spiritual side of our make-up, we tend to dismiss it. The Biblical Link to Addiction and Recovery will initially concentrate its primary focus on the spiritual root and the corresponding fruits, which we know as 'active addiction' where, the primary need of everyone concerned is the arrest and reversal of various processes in which the various players find themselves trapped:

- The addict will be in a process of promising, trying and failing

- The family will be in a process of expecting, judging and blaming

A neutral ground needs to be established with an atmosphere of acceptance and compassion. This will contribute immensely towards negating the inter-personal hostility and unreasonable expectations. From there a joint effort can be made to establishing a recovery-focused direction. Looking for someone or something to blame will not offer us a solution. The addicted individual does not necessarily make their initial choice to use, abuse and booze because of things like bad parenting or some hidden abuse issues. For many, by simply exploring the options of trying 'something more', they follow their underdeveloped logic and self-belief and naively decide simply to try using addictive chemicals.

There are those who suffered at the hands of abusive parents, siblings and other family members. Many addicts who have passed through our care experienced horrific treatment even under the 'care' of religious figures and school teachers. It happens.

However, two wrongs never made anything right. That is the doctrine of the devil himself. Therefore drinking or drugging oneself to death because of some previous evil influence must never be made to sound right. Addicts come from every level of society. We frequently identify that there is one deadly common denominator between all who eventually become chemically dependent. Years of counseling hundreds of addicts, in prisons, in hospitals, on street corners, in Churches, in cardboard boxes and in 12-bedroomed mansions, no matter the color, creed or background, at root level they each believed the same fundamental self-deception: "I can drink, take or smoke this potion, pill or poisonous chemical, but I will not become addicted, I will surely not die".

This mindset is known as the 'addictive denial'. However, if for a moment we explore this 'addictive logic' a little further, we see that it quickly cancels itself out because there are millions of other individuals with the same belief, who also experiment with and recreationally use various forms of mind and mood altering chemicals, who do not go on to become addicted.

If the addicted individual is, as this book now suggests, under a 'spiritually deceptive government' as opposed to a 'deadly diseased design', trying to combat an inaccurately diagnosed 'disease' with a 'deception' flavored solution, no matter how philosophically or psychologically fine sounding, can only ever lead to a temporary hope and an inevitable increase of despair.

The truth is simple: people can start taking drugs for any one of a variety of reasons, but then find themselves unable to stop for an accumulation of other reasons.

Taking this argument one step further, I would even suggest that this 'deception' principle could very easily be in active application even within the foundational ethos of many of the worlds sought after Addiction Treatment Clinics if they dogmatically promote the Disease concept.

Addicts very often voicelessly settle for a fragile second-hand identity from 12-Step membership, based on a lack of obvious chaos and what look like signs of 'development' and 'change' which naturally takes place as a result of simply being chemical free. It is true, a process of emotional development does begin at the removal of the chemicals, but we must take into consideration the condition of the person when their developmental process stopped, and not fall into the trap of thinking that abstinence from the chemicals equates to being clean and sober. Whether deceived or diseased, the chemically dependent person comes out of an addiction emotionally younger than when they went in into it. There is a propensity within them to become like the people they mix with in order to establish an identity for themselves. Likewise, members of the 12-Step Recovery Community have their own way of talking and greeting, socializing and watching out for each other. I want to suggest that individuals coming out of chemical dependencies do not have to settle for this 12 Step self-help second-hand identity in order to stay clean and sober. I would, in fact, warn those in early recovery against resigning themselves to 12 Step memberships for the rest of their lives and to set targets of independence from the day they start to develop.

As a foundation for my argument of addiction having Biblical roots, I feel it would be helpful if we could attempt a journey into the root systems of both addicts and contemporary treatment models with a goal of mutual recognition. The Biblical Link to Addiction and Recovery hopes to open windows of spiritual illumination into the intentions, hopes, beliefs and poisonously protective defense mechanisms of an ever increasing sub-culture of addicts and their families, offering an alternative diagnosis to that of the being 'diseased'.

In order to launch my argument, I want to suggest an alternative approach to the treatment of an addiction than that of the very common belief that addictions are a 'disease', primarily rooted in 'the great lie'. The following statement is what is known as the great lie: 'If you saw the real me you would not like me'. I want to suggest, with Biblical support, that this statement is possibly actually one of the greatest truths any individual could (a) discover, (b) accept and (c) reveal about themselves. So to call this statement the great lie, is, I believe, a deceptive belief.

1. Because you might not like the real me I use chemicals – Is avoiding the truth

2. To get clean I have to become someone you approve of – Is shifting responsibility

3. If you will not like me I cannot get clean – Is playing the blame game

To a dying individual with a severe identity crisis, the secular approach actually makes a deep degree of sense. It could be described as attractively seductive and temporarily satiating if offered to a starving and searching spirituality, especially if the only other apparent alternative is a return to active destructive addiction, jails, institutions and death. From this platform the 'diseased' individual must therefore seek out and settle for reliance upon other, like-minded 'diseased' individuals in order to achieve any sense of acceptance, direction, belonging and growth. Criteria for membership of this 'recovery community' are also attractively simple: One must simply profess 'the desire to stop using' and then 'keep coming back, it only works if you work it'[1].

Temptation instantly looms within a large portion of Christian mindsets at this point with an urge to 'theologize' our battle cry: 'It's not by might, nor by power, but My Spirit say's The Lord". Whilst that is very true, it means nothing to the lost, so I would therefore recommend the purchase and study of 'Chemical Dependency Counselling' by Robert Perkinson[2].

Speaking of the contemporary epidemic belief that the need is to heal the 'poor self-image', in his book 'Beyond Seduction' Dave Hunt points out: 'One of the Bible's major purposes is to correct man's high view of himself', asking 'how can creatures whose besetting sin is thinking too highly of themselves ever be convinced that their problem is in fact a low self-esteem[3]?

The journey to the roots of any addiction will involve much reliance upon the findings of Professor Perkinson and the well of genius within the World Health Organization and beyond, to whom millions of addicts and families owe immeasurable debts of gratitude. However, for the duration of this particular journey, let us shed even our highest regard of man that we may be empowered truly to seek development in the spiritual realm of our being. Let's just pray to God that we might see through spiritual eyes; an understandable, applicable alternative to

---

1. Opening and closing mantra's of (English) 12 Step Recovery Meetings.
2. Stage Publications, ISBN 0-7619-2388-8
3. Beyond Seduction, Harvest House Publishers 1987, page 13.

the definitions of man about men and that we might identify and accept that when God made man in His image, He did not make little god's. He made independently dependent personalities with whom He desired intimacy in relationship. They, in turn, would develop under His influence and He simply desired expressions of desires for His continued influence, development and provision based on the truth of His Word. The inevitable result of 'His Will' being fulfilled could only therefore be that they individually develop theologically and thereby display reflections (*imagery*) of Him. We therefore, the created being, must forfeit any inclinations within us to define this God, and seek humbly that He allow us light enough to see that He alone can offer true definition of Himself and of man.

In his book 'The Life of Paul[4], F.B. Meyer, reflecting on man's disconnected spiritual condition said: 'Contrary to what we usually think, the source of a stream must not be sought where it arises in some green pasture among the hills where the mountain sheep come to drink, but in the mighty sea that is drawn up in evaporation or in the clouds that condense against the close slopes of the hills. So too is it with regard to the life of God within us. In it's infancy we are apt to suppose it originated in our will and choice that we return to our Father's house'. If we continue in the same vein, addressing our spiritual life as that of flowing waters, and 'The Father's House' being His Oceanic Spiritual Kingdom, my aim is to travel back up stream to seek out and plunge into the darkest stagnant ponds of addiction in an attempt to empower spiritual shipwrecks lying dying and seemingly no good in the mud of failed recovery attempts and serial relapsing, with life-changing information of a Trinitarian salvage company.

In order to present adequately a foundational argument for a Biblical Link to Addiction and Recovery, we must be willing to undertake an examination of the text and the spiritual and behavioral examples for humanity as they are set out in the story of our Biblical parents of Genesis chapter 2, Adam and Eve.

If you take up 5 different commentaries on the creation story set out in Genesis, you may come away confused, with 5 different exegetical views of what it all means and what the various words mean in Hebrew

---

4. The Life of Paul, Emerald Books (Washington) 1995, page 9.

and in Greek. For the purpose of this exercise, therefore, I just want to ask this question: What does The Bible say about God, you and me?

This we know: Genesis 1.

God created, inspected, and declared, and therefore it is written ...

1. The light was good Genesis 1:4

2. The earth and the seas were good Genesis 1:10

3. The grass, the herbs, the trees and the fruit were good Genesis 1:12

4. The sun and the moon and the stars were good Genesis 1:18

5. The whales and creatures from the waters and every winged fowl were good Genesis 1:21

6. The cattle and every thing that creeps upon the earth were good Genesis 1:25

Genesis 1:28

God blessed Adam and Eve, and God said unto them, "be fruitful and multiply, replenish the earth, and subdue it; have dominion over the fish of the sea, and over the fowl of the air, and over every living thing that moves upon the earth".

Then ...

7. God saw everything that he had made, and, behold, it was very good Genesis 1:31

So there they were, saturated in God's goodness, given dominion, with no concept of evil.

There were no thorns at this point, there was no relational discord, and there was no such a question as 'how are you today'? Everything God had made was indeed 'very good'. There was no alternative of 'not ok'. They had perfect harmony, connection and communication with God, each other and with everything that God had made upon and within the earth and everything from within the seas. Neither man nor beast knew anything of fear or of danger, all was one, all was safe. God walked in the garden in the cool of the day and they existed within the eternally developmental influence of their relationship with Him within His original divine design. Water will have been of the purest, freshest quality ever known to man. Fruit will have been of the purest, sweetest quality ever known to man. The air they breathed will have been of the purest and most refreshing quality ever known to man. The joy of intimately knowing God and that His pleasure and absolute blessing rested upon them will have been of the highest and of the deepest of delights ever known to man. Not even the Angels of Heaven are anywhere recorded as ever having such a quality and depth of connection and interaction with this awesome God, who is forever God over everything that He has created, majestic in power, infinite yet intimate, all seeing, all knowing, all powerful.

Genesis 2:16-17 "The Lord God commanded the man saying, 'Of every tree of the garden you may feel free to eat; but of the tree of knowledge of good and evil you shall not eat, for in the day that you eat of it you shall surely die'".

This commandment was revealed by God to the man. His role at that time therefore was to carry God's Word into his relationship with his wife and to govern the created order. That made him 'Prophet and King in the home and throughout the earth' - a Prophet is one who makes a verbal understandable declaration of a divinely given revelation. We have no written record of whether or not Adam relayed the 'thou shalt not eat' revelation of God's Word verbatim to his wife or whether he placed his own interpretation of what he had been told, but on close inspection of the that which is written we soon see a slight deviation from The Word within the prophets constituency:

Genesis 3:1-4 Now the serpent was more cunning than any beast of the field which The Lord God had made. And he said to the woman, "Has God indeed said 'You shall not eat of every tree of the garden'?" And the woman said to the serpent, "We may eat the fruit of the trees of the garden, but of the fruit of the tree which is in the midst of the garden; God has said, 'You shall not eat it, nor shall you touch it lest you die'.

Many theologians argue that the man was right next to his wife at the time of this discussion. I would argue against this stance because (a) text does not tell us this (b) devilish attack has since proved itself to be cowardly and divisive. Therefore, I would suggest, isolated from her husband and still void of any knowledge of evil, the vulnerable lady becomes seductively embroiled in a debate about the rights and wrongs of God's Word. It would appear that the purpose of the debate from the side of the serpent was to attack the defenseless mind of the woman and to make right sound wrong. If he could succeed in making right sound wrong, the only logical conclusion left to her would be that wrong must actually be right. Once this was achieved the temptation became 'not to fully rest upon God's Word as He has chosen to deliver it'.

God had recently commanded the man to 'cultivate the garden' in Gen. 2:15. We are not shown any form of debate between Adam and Eve with regard to the instructions of how to cultivate it or of the commandment not to eat from the tree of knowledge of good and evil. However, common sense tells us if touching any of the trees had carried deadly consequences, God would have surely said so in His horticultural instruction. That's what this True and Living God does, He says what He means and He means what He says and His Word brings and sustains life and it protects and it provides for His children.

Because there was no such thing as insincerity at that point, and because Adam and Eve had no such thing as hindsight to learn from, I believe we may trust that Eve was guiltier of naiveté than she was of willful rebellion. This first daughter of The Most High God, the absolute apple of His eye, displays a sincere desire to protect and support that which 'she thought' to be God's Word in the face of humanity's first recorded interaction with the deceptive power of evil.

However, even if we do allow ourselves to conclude that Eve had sincere protective intensions, she still not only failed to rest upon God's Word, she actually added to it. We are not told of the existence of discord of any kind prior to this unfortunate incident, so everything was good with Eve, but only as long as everything was good with Eve. Once the tempter pollutes the purity of her naive heart and mind, the following dynamics come into play:

1. That which was right in accordance to pure doctrine was made to sound wrong.

2. That which was wrong in accordance to false doctrine was made to sound right.

We see a spiral of belief, attitude and behaviour:

Genesis 3:8 "And they heard the sound of The Lord God walking in the garden in the cool of the day, and Adam and his wife <u>hid themselves from the presence of The Lord God</u> among the trees of the garden"

Genesis 3:11 "Have you eaten from the tree of which I commanded you that you should not eat"?

Genesis 3:12-13 "The woman whom you gave to be with me, she gave to me of the tree and I ate. And The Lord said to the woman, "What is this that you have done"? And the woman said "The serpent deceived me and I ate"

1. They believe they can hide from God

2. Neither of them take personal responsibility

3. The blame game begins

Q. Why would someone try to hide from a Loving, All-seeing, All-knowing Father? A. Because of a polluted perception of the truth, 'I have failed, I am bad, and I must be punished'

If we have not yet recognized yet truly want to find The Biblical Link to Addiction, we must now take up a Bible and honestly consider the big-picture:

In isolation from the God-appointed authoritative leadership, in the face of an unrecognizable spiritual enemy, overestimating the ability of the self to discern right from wrong, leading to an inaccurate exegesis of God's Will, we see development of the mould for the following spiritual and psychological blue-print for the rest of humanity:

1. They fear that God's Word won't be enough
   – Genesis 3:3

2. They become susceptible to spiritual deception
   – 1 Timothy 2:14

3. They start to believe that God is unforgiving
    – Genesis 3:7

4. They attempt to cover up the damage   –
    Genesis 3:7

5. They attempt to hide from the truth
    – Genesis 3:8

6. They avoid taking personal responsibility
    – Genesis 3:10

7. They instinctively play the blame game
    – Genesis 3:12

Now see if you can identify the very same poisonous principles of this progression in the following statement from an imaginary parent regarding an imaginary addicted teenage daughter:

"She won't go to Church, she will not admit that there is a problem, whatever we tell her she does the opposite, she's always mixing with the wrong people and covering for them with lies and whenever we confront her over anything she storms out of the house and somehow manages to leave everyone else feeling guilty".

Not so difficult to imagine, is it? The Addictive Spiritual DNA - Born in Eden.

The wonderful thing is, if we continue to peer through the Biblical lens, or better still, a Biblical kaleidoscope, we will also catch a glimpse of God's Fatherly nature. We frequently see His obvious desire for a relationship with His wayward children. The Divine Heart is not only clearly seen throughout text as holding the desire for reconciliation at its core; we are even given a glimpse of an urge to run and embrace a smelly wayward child from a pig-pen. This is the recorded truth of the nature of the very same God from whom Adam and Eve had tried to hide. This is also the truth of how little they truly understood of Him, even before their hearts and minds had fallen prey to deception and division. So if you or someone you know complains of feeling far from God and/or find His Word difficult to understand, rest assured, you're in good company and you're actually not to blame. The distance between you and God is not as vast as it might sometimes seem; it may just indicate that there are some things in your life that need to go.

CHAPTER FOUR

THE FIRST POTENTIAL ALCOHOLIC

If we travel back to that fatefully defining day in Eden, before the serpent entered the scene, we must see two human beings as they were, in perfect peace, with this Father God. Not only did they lack knowledge of evil, they even lacked the ability to imagine what the world would look like with anything evil in it. They knew God in a very personal and intimate way, and they therefore knew of the goodness of being in harmony with God. As the morning lark sounded at the dawning of every peaceful day in Eden, Adam will not have even been in any need to yawn. The earth's natural resources were at their very purest and there will not have been one atom of pollution in the oxygen that they breathed. A yawn is a reflex to a need for more oxygen to the bloodstream. A reflex is a built-in physical reaction over which people do not have control. Adam and Eve had dominion in the earth, they were in complete control. A yawn is also associated with people being under stress or bored or over- worked, Adam and Eve knew of no such concepts. If they did sleep, they surely woke in need of nothing, with a song in the soul. How can we best explain the spiritual and psychological condition at that point? Adams whole character was in complete harmony with God, with his fellow man and with everything in creation. To ask at that time, 'how are you?' would only create humanity's first predicament, because it went without saying that they were continually 'at-one'.

Life at that time brought with it an inner assurance of love, acceptance and significance and the world around them held its own (seemingly) incorruptible social security. How could they have ever foreseen such atrocities as babies being abandoned at birth, incest, rape, incestual-rape, prostitution, murder and suicide, mass murder and/or mass suicide? How could they have anticipated teenage girls cutting themselves with razor blades in an effort to create a connection between their self-disgust, an internal turmoil and a twisted logic? How could they, in their wildest dreams, ever have even begun to anticipate that the future could hold heartbreaking stories of regular young men performing lewd sex acts in unclean public lavatories on members of the same sex for money, to buy a powder that they would ritualistically 'cook-up' and inject into their bloodstreams in a blind search for that long lost Eden-state of euphoric being? How could they have anticipated the millions of their direct ancestors being gassed and burned in concentration camps, men, women and babies alike? Yet as we follow onward from Genesis 3:23 *"So the Lord God sent them out of the Garden of Eden"* - we start to see a dying humanity, under God's judgment, relationally and spiritually detached from its divine life source and, we must surely imagine, a broken hearted Father, unable to pollute His righteousness by controlling their choices, evicting them from His garden. There they find themselves, on the outside looking in, with no natural knowledge of evil and an unrecognizable need to develop an understanding as to how to handle vulnerability, disconnection and neediness. Surely they will have soon started to develop humanity's first haunting sense of failure and loss and a fear of the unknown world in front of them. How did they recognize and harness the new urges to resent each other, without eyes to identify the root problems or adequate terminologies to express and release what would soon become their negative emotional driving forces?

Unknown to them, the whole of the created order had been turned on its environmental, spiritual, emotional and relational head. Whereas God's children naturally grew to become more and more like Him simply through their reception of His divine influence upon them without fear, shame or thorns, Adam's children, as we shall see, go on to become everything their parents disapprove of and, in turn, they then have to teach their offspring how not to make the mistakes they made. This principle is still very much alive today to the extent of millions of parents, still evolving backwards, making it their life's goal to turn their children into what they themselves failed to become. Can you hear the serpent laughing?

For Adam and Eve, their once perfect environment had now taken on a bi-polar type change with its painfully extreme daytime heat and contrasting night time cold. The Middle Eastern wilderness must have felt terribly hostile to these two 'dependently independent' characters now exiled from the source of their initial security, identity and development. Now, for the first time, mankind finds itself struggling with 'needs' to meet. Life outside of Eden demanded a specific type, strength and quality of character which would be required for them to survive. That character would have to be developed through the struggle and the failure and what would surely be a seemingly inexplicable emotional volatility within the search for the necessary balance and relational harmony that constitutes a healthy marriage. I believe it would be safe to assume that Adam would have regularly found himself holding his head in his hands in despair, probably somewhere quiet out in that rugged wilderness. He may well have had specific caves or rocks to which he would retreat and reflect on the difficulties of life and the opportunities lost. I would imagine even he would have been shocked at the intensity of his emotional explosions when the nature to blame took over in times of relational difficulty. I wonder how they managed the alien emotions that only exist because of divine loss. How would Eve have known how to recognize or handle her monthly cycle and the hormonal hurricane which will have crept into their relationship? What did Adam make of going off to the office with a kiss, then coming home to deafening silence; or going to sleep in relational good-books, but waking up in the dog-house?

They had no hindsight to fall back on; how did they learn to understand and deal with life's intricacies like tooth decay, hair loss and wrinkles?

These insidious pressures of a deteriorating life were literally beyond human comprehension. How would they have coped when Eve discovered she was pregnant? She had no one to explain to her what "the pains of childbirth" really meant, so imagine her first fear-filled confusions around her first contractions and her frustrations with a husband who only seemed to grow in uselessness right before her eyes! The only viable explanation for their survival as husband and wife during those tumultuous times will have been a returning to their relationship with God. I think it fair to say that when the physical side of her pregnancy got to that excruciating time for Eve, Adam's primary role will have been that of a humble praying husband. Their first born child surely will have brought an immense sense of achievement and joy into their world, and their initial focus will have been on this new life; but we must observe and learn from Eve as she exhibits role model qualities of what we today would call 'Christian parenting' when, at Cain's birth, she gives glory to God: "I have acquired a man from The Lord" – Gen. 4:1.

They then start to experience the wonders of examining this tiny reproduction of themselves. Counting his little fingers and toes, and marveling at his funny little noises and facial expressions. Surely mom and dad will have simply sunk into that marvelously mysterious miracle quietly suckling on her breast, and very probably even wept at this wondrous new gift from God. Surely the magnificence of this miniature reflection of him will have stirred within them an inner sense of inadequacy towards the parental task ahead. What painful lessons they would learn from parenting through their inexplicably deep feelings of love and protection towards this little one! Would it not then slowly start to dawn on them how Father God once felt those exact same feelings, and more, towards them? How Adam's quiet times must have changed once he started to view life through a Father's eyes. What reflections will Adam have undergone as Cain started to grow in his individuality and Eve started to say, 'Oh he grows more and more like you every day', and each time she said it, he would be forgiven for re-feeling his grief at the thought of his lost opportunity to grow more in the likeness of his Father God. For that was the plan.

Maybe it was when Adam started to understand how the new life before him, the production of his seed, needed to be watched and nurtured, cherished and nourished or it would die, that the penny really started to drop. Maybe only then did Adam start to see that God had not made little self-sustaining gods when He created man, but that man could only ever reproduce man through procreation and pain, which will forever be in need of divine reconnection, provision and care or it will die.

Now fast forward a little while. Imagine Cain as he reaches the terrible two's, pushing the boundaries of his exhausted dad, challenging his authority and pushing him to the outer limits of his emotional and hitherto unexplored psychological make-up. Imagine that first smacked bottom and the sobbing child. Imagine the aching father's heart, because although the punishment may have been necessary, perhaps out of natural tiredness it was too harsh and guilt haunts the struggling parent.

Hindsight now starts to take on a 20-20 quality for Adam and Eve and surely their own behaviour towards God will have gradually come into focus. Like any parent, Adam and Eve will have known that they actually know more about the child than the child knew about himself, and once again, Adam will have been put in touch with his futility of trying to hide from God. It was probably in moments of solitude and reflection that a search took place to find the words adequate enough to describe the essence of God's protective Father Heart and the reality of man's depravity. Maybe during his search for sanity he started to pass down the generations the truth of man's vulnerability before the eyes of The Living God, which will have been passed on and on until several thousands of years later, King David, "a man after God's own heart" (Acts 13:22) reached for his quill and recorded the following conclusion:

Psalm 139:1-18

Lord, you have examined me and you know me. You know everything I do; from far away you understand all my thoughts. You see me, whether I am working or resting; you know all my actions. Even before I speak, you already know what I will say. You are all around me on every side; you protect me with your power. Your knowledge of me is too deep; it is beyond my understanding. Where could I go to escape from you? Where could I get away from your presence? If I went up to heaven, you would be there; if I lay down in the world of the dead, you would be there. If I flew away beyond the east or lived in the farthest place in the west, you would be there to lead me, you would be there to help me. I could ask the darkness to hide me or the light around me to turn into night, but even darkness is not dark for you, and the night is as bright as the day. Darkness and light are the same to you. You created every part of me; you put me together in my mother's womb. I praise you because you are to be feared; all you do is strange and wonderful. I know it with all my heart. When my bones were being formed, carefully put together in my mother's womb, when I was growing there in secret, you knew that I was there - you saw me before I was born. The days allotted to me had all been recorded in your book, before any of them ever began. O God, how difficult I find your thoughts; how many of them there are! If I counted them, they would be more than the grains of sand. When I awake, I am still with you.

And let's not forget, in the midst of these periods of relational and developmental chaos, these first human beings would also have had the same dark spirit of deception and division to contend with. The Deceiver's role being that of deceiving, dividing and accusing; he deceives man about the truth of God's Word, strives to pollute and divide the marriage and the family and he accuses man before God.

Cain is born, and then Able, and straight away we see children whose names are still globally synonymous with envy, violence and murder. But once again, if we examine the events around this first murder scene in Genesis 4:1-10 and try to imagine what Adam saw, we must only grow in compassion for this man, through whom sin made its entrance into the world. Imagine the emotional and psychological chaos as the body of the second son hit the ground with blood gushing from an open skull. Adam and Eve suddenly find themselves thrust into humanity's very first state of 'how can this be? How difficult will it have been for Adam to give God worship and praise throughout these days of death, decay and loss? Who did they have to teach them about the need to grieve? How would they cope with the overwhelming depression which follows this tragic and brutal loss of life? Would Adam now catch another glimpse of God's broken heart over the day that they themselves tried to hide from Him, thereby choosing the way of death?

Now step back in time and visit the hostile heat of the Middle-eastern wilderness. Allow yourself to stumble across a heartbroken and confused Adam as he wrestles with the way things have turned out and his corresponding emotional misery. With your gift of hindsight, would you not believe yourself to have a complete understanding if you found him sitting at his child's graveside, haunted by his sense of failure as God's child, as Eve's husband and now even as the dead boy's parent. Would some of you not even quietly sob with him? He will most surely be trying to make sense of humanity's very first dilemma: 'I don't know which way to turn for the best'. If you stand back and watch from a distance, I believe you'll probably see him periodically bursting into uncontrollable convulsions of sobbing and frustration at the mess within him and around him. Not only so, I believe it reasonable to surmise and imagine these foundational struggles. I actually feel it probable that most of us could add some struggles of our own to intensify the torment. However, as you do, please try to do so with gratitude in your heart towards God, because in His graciousness He minimized our life span to a mere "three-score years and ten" - Psalm 90 (approximately 70 years). Not so for Adam - he had over 900 years of this developing insanity to endure where 'every intension of the heart of man was only evil continually" - Genesis 6:5!

With that in mind, let's imagine again that we find Adam 850 years into his exile and torment. Go and sit next to him in his rocky place of isolation during one of his depressions. Witness the tears in his eyes and the shrugs of hopelessness as he rocks back and forth in an effort to comfort himself. Quietly place an arm around his shoulder and try telling him of how 'you understand his pain and his frustration'. Do you really think he would be able to believe you or receive solace from your sympathy? ...

"HOW CAN ANYONE REALLY UNDERSTAND WHAT I AM GOING THROUGH"?

Now try the following experiment: pour him a nice cold beer straight from the fridge with a thousand droplets of condensation clinging to the outside of the glass. Hold it up to the light to display the beautiful golden liquid within the glass and then pass it to him and invite him to drink. Then just sit back and watch the influence it has over how he thinks and feels about life, and I believe that it will be right there, right at that first point of contact, in the secret vault of his innermost being, you will see humanity's first potential alcoholic. If further confirmation be needed, do another experiment: just give him the one drink and then walk out of his life. Leave him for 25 years, and then return. What aspect of your initial meeting with him do you think will be the first thing to spring to his mind on your return? How long do you think it would be before he approached the subject and asked: 'you got any more of that drink'? I would confidently suggest that the drink would be his primary memory when he sees you; and just as a seal of confirmation that we are probably talking about the planet's very first potentially chemically dependent person, watch the excitement grow from within him when you tell him: "the earth naturally produces it". Any observing addiction therapist would connect these preoccupations and reactions to what we now call 'the addictive personality' and/or 'chemical dependency'.

If only they had recognized and trusted that their growth, security and significance for life could rest fully in the truth of The Word of God. We would all still be in Eden, right would still be right, nothing would be wrong, and we would each be living in freedom from those developmentally restrictive instincts and self-deceptions about who we are and who we are not and about who God is or who He is not. Evil would be something miserably existing in a dungeon of its own eternal suffering and there would be a sign on the door, written in Hebrew, clearly stating: "No Entry for Human Beings".

CHAPTER FIVE

THE ROAD TO RUIN

Experimentation

Driving along the coast of South Africa in my 4x4, my phone starts to play Sam Cooke's *'Everybody Likes to Cha Cha Cha'*. I press the little button on the side of the device attached to my ear and I answer the call from Nic, an ex-army buddy, phoning from his office in Stoke on the far side of planet earth in England. I open the conversation by telling him how the temperature gauge in my car tells me that it is a blistering 41 degrees outside. We share some friendly banter about the weather and about that weekend's game at Old Trafford where Michael Owen scored in the final minute of extra time against Manchester City to win the game for United. We share a few jokes about our blue rivals and with roars of laughter our international interaction comes to end. I take the car up to just below the speed limit, flick it into cruise control, switch the air-con on and kick my shoes off. I settle back to enjoy the drive to the sound of my favorite CD, 'Unshackled', worship songs from Keswick. As I drive, I sing and pray. Welcome to 2010, our age of the quick-fix and instant gratification where the world now defines for itself that which is right and that which is wrong. Planet earth has become a place where 'normal' is where it is acceptable to sell deadly and destructive addictive substances like nicotine and alcohol to other human beings, knowing it will kill them. Not only so, it is also perfectly acceptable to target our children subliminally in the marketing of these poisons by making them look like the rite of passage into adulthood. Parents are guaranteed that the seductive influences of the chemical culture will be made to look alluring and it is only a case of 'when' that it will beckon every one of our defenseless teenagers. I call them defenseless because this onslaught begins before they reach 'maturity' – the age where they should have some degree of knowledge of good and evil. However, because the chemical culture persistently winks at them through what the world has made to be 'social joviality' – many of them are deceived and never reach any degree of maturity. They fall for the offering of 'impressive' personality changes within the sub-culture of chemical dependency. Any newsreel from anywhere in the world on any given day will give out graphic details of how youngsters are getting addicted, overdosing, stabbing each other, raping and in many cases going to prison for the rest of their life. Good kids from good stock, seduced into a life that actually hastens death. The facts are there for all to see, but from somewhere within the teenager, they have this belief "you shall surely not die".

There is a 'deceptive influence' brought on by mind- and mood-altering chemicals, the most prolific being at first point of contact. Ask any alcoholic what they got from their first interaction with alcohol; get them to reflect and explore precisely what took place within their personality a few seconds after the alcohol entered their system. Despite the fact that few, if any, will say how they actually enjoyed the immediate consumption experience, all will agree how the unpleasant effects of the taste were soon forgotten as the 'influence' of the chemical 'took over'. Therefore it was not *'the chemical going in'* that they became attracted to, it was *'the influence that took over them',* and in the final analysis all invariably agree how they *'received'* a shift in their personality. This shift was predominantly made up of what turned out to be counterfeit and temporary sensations of Euphoria, Significance and Security.

I have become more and more convinced that the age of the paranoid parent is upon us. As addiction specialists, we receive countless phone calls from parents in panic. We even get teenagers sent to our rehab because both parents have slipped into lying awake at night worrying. Many times, during family meetings at one of our facilities, the mom will reveal: "whilst I was cleaning his room, I found this in his shoe" – and some form of drug paraphernalia will have been discovered. Invariably we then hear: 'he's also been drinking too much and mixing with the wrong crowd for some time now'.

The Biblical Link to Addiction and Recovery suggests that we take a step back from cleaning the inside of our teenager's shoes and playing the blame game and take another look. If you believe that someone you love is involved in some form of dangerous chemical activity, please try to focus on that personality, as opposed to the volumes of chemicals you believe they are using and the quality of the types of people they are mixing with. The progressive chaos is not going to make sense until we slow down and establish the right questions with regard to the individual involved and the spiritual, psychological and emotional condition they were in at their first point of contact. The problem of drug usage must never be approached as being created by 'peer pressure' or too rapidly categorized as being 'an addiction'.

We need to localize the problem and ask ourselves two questions:

1. What type of personality *gives in* to peer pressure'?

2. What happens to this person when they first consumed the chemical?

Peer pressure must never be addressed as the problem, that's exactly what the potential addict wants you to think. *Giving in* to the peer pressure, that's the problem. For many, on experimentation day, the 'chemical influence' felt like a coming out of a wilderness type of experience. They seemingly moved from their unidentified unsettled condition, into what they falsely perceive to be a place of arrival. However, in reality, contrary to the seemingly wonderful sense of fulfillment offered by the chemical, a very subtle process of deadly decay was conceived. The psychological essence of this decay sounds something like this: *'with an increasing ease, that which we know to be wrong starts to sound right, as that which we know to be right slowly starts sounding wrong'.*

The Biblical Link to Addiction and Recovery suggests that this 'inside-out-morality' to be the spiritual and psychological DNA of the potentially chemically dependent personality. All that therefore remains is to run this 'new found personality' through the wringer backwards in order to establish precisely what kind of individual it really was who gave in to peer pressure and settled for this counterfeit identity.

It is widely accepted that the chemical 'offers the user something', therefore, whatever it brings must have been absent prior to intake. I have frequently seen three common denominating conditions highlighted by an enormous number of struggling addicts coming in to our safe therapeutic environment who are asked the following question: "What did the chemical bring into your life at the start of your using?" Many of them describe how they received feelings of

Euphoria, Significance and Security. As we then investigate further and ask how they really felt about themselves and about their life prior to that first chemical intake, they very often start to cry. They slowly start to see how the chemical influence only ever really offered them a counterfeit opposite of how they really felt about themselves.

1. The antonym of Euphoria? – Dreary

2. The antonym of Significance? – Unimportant

3. The antonym of Security? – Lost

On the whole, I have found that most chemically dependent people feel this way about themselves and most of them had transferred that belief onto their life to come, before they started to die under the influence of the chemical. They also seem to share another very common belief-thread which served to solidify this negative foundational self-belief and which was an added belief of how, 'the way they felt before they started using the chemicals was wrong'. Internal dialogue therefore sounds like this: 'I must be wrong because I have wrong feelings'.

Therefore, at First Point of Contact (FPC) with the influence of a chemical, our user experiences what really feels like a spiritual awakening, and for the potential addict, this 'awakening' is the moment of conception. Although the monster within is only in its embryonic state at FPC, its negative development is thereafter unstoppable as long as it remains unidentified and/or denied. The whole mindset of the pregnant one gradually starts to find it easier to turn right into wrong and wrong into right. For instance, in the event of the primary chemical being a legally restricted substance such as cocaine, this spiritual awakening is immediately supported by a criminal rationale of: 'I'm only buying it; I'm not guilty of any crime', which in and of itself, tells us what form of 'spirit' we have 'awakened'.

So we see the outbreak of war between the mind, the desires and the conscience. The conscience yearns to keep right right, but the deceptive mind somehow seems to develop an arsenal of justifications

32

and rationalizations for its shameful and potentially deadly choices. The process of time sees a dying conscience and growth in intolerance towards the truth. Not only does the mind become more and more comfortable with deceptive thinking, it will also think in ways which support the cravings for more of the chemical, or for approval, or for romance, sex, power, finance. The list is sadly endless.

By entertaining the counterfeit spirituality, in the recreational phase, our potential addict unknowingly removes himself from his natural process of growth and development. It is just as if someone has pointed a remote control at the emotional process of the potential addict and pressed 'slow motion'. The self-deceiving addict actually believes himself to be in 'fast forward' because of the counterfeit feelings of omniscience and omnipotence. The truth is, he is deceived and blinded and will very soon cross a line in his drug using where his whole personality will go into an emotionally developmental pause under the stranglehold of chemical dependency.

CHAPTER SIX

RECREATION

From the day that this false and temporary spiritual 'connection' is made, for the potential addict the influence of that first high lingers within the heart of the desires very much in the same way as Juliet will have lingered in Romeo's heart following his first point of contact with her. That initial intensity of influence given by the chemical at FPC will persistently be sought thereafter, yet never actually found. Because active addiction in a behavioural sense does not manifest itself at FPC there could be a long period of incubation, much in the same way that Malaria does not immediately follow the mosquito bite; so too active destructive addiction will not immediately follow FPC. The chemical user can in no way ever anticipate the life-consuming power of addiction and in his heart he will sincerely believe that he will never become "like those alcoholics or heroin addicts". However, in a spiritual sense, dreams and ambitions get sabotaged by these self-deceptions and life suddenly stands on the precipice of a nightmare. We have no way of seeing that something far more serious than a chemical intake has actually taken place. A potential addict will take part in the normal day to day functioning of his life, going to work, the gym, and sporting activities at the weekends. Even the closest family members will remain unaware of the conceived cancerous seed of decay germinating within. Early stirrings of the conceived monster are impossible to identify without hindsight. Everything looks to be quite normal, but slowly, for the carrier, the week starts to take on a new 'feel'. A new sense of excitement starts to well up as the weekend approaches. To the potential addict, increasing pre-occupations creep in about the impending rendezvous with this 'new friend'. In a very subtle way, the user starts experiencing very similar thoughts and feelings that young lovers experience in those early blossomings of a romantic relationship. As the weekend nears, our user drifts into a feel-good zone wherein he experiences feelings of friendliness towards almost everyone and he suddenly seems to have an exaggerated zest for life. He himself will not fully understand what is going on because of the lack of knowledge of evil and the condition of self-deception; neither would he acknowledge the truth – that this 'natural' high is an anticipatory reaction to an impending chemical intake - if it were presented to him in surround-sound.

Work colleagues will start to detect an obnoxious air about him as the secret he is keeping slowly starts to develop within him, changing him.

The truth looks like this: all his relationships start taking on a counterfeit sincerity as the self-deception slowly 'matures' into arrogance, invincibility, irresponsibility and immaturity.

A protective mental deflection routine will increasingly manifest itself within the daily life of a potential addict, even in these days of incubation. Any conversation about the dangers or the stupidity of drug using will be minimized, even ridiculed and laughed off, but in the process of time, as the developing monster grows, the reactions will gradually become hostile. If the individual is not approached with discernment – the eyes to see the difference between good and evil – even with the highest of moral intensions, we can easily force him into defensive isolation. The danger then changes from a genuine concern for his well-being, into a desire to prove a point; and before anyone realizes what is happening, we find ourselves engaged in a power struggle which will only then exacerbate the seedling monster within.

We simply cannot panic.

Whilst loved ones need a unified empowerment in their struggle to help the potential addict, they need to understand that if their strength is to be of any benefit, it must be rooted in humility, not desires for revenge or fear. The primary purpose of the worried family at this initial intervention is the sabotage of the progress of the deceptive thinking within the user. We must turn the potentially problematic individual into becoming the means of a solution. By the time concerns are rising within family members, the user will also be having several of his own in the form of niggling suspicions that something is not quite right anymore.

The potential addict should be invited to a family meeting. If we can get everyone into a relaxed frame of mind we will make the most progress. Try to create as relaxed an atmosphere as is possible and then when the mood is almost jovial, let the senior family member invite the gathering to convene as a meeting. Maybe, in an ideal situation, get a brother or sister to get alongside the potential addict and gently hold his hand or place an arm around his shoulder. Each family member must try to lay aside any personal hurts, fears or opinions and should try to display their love and concern toward the potentially problematic individual.

Relaxing Empowerment

"Some of your recent behaviour has created a concern in us. We have each noticed a change in you. You just don't seem yourself. So we took the liberty of seeking advice and it looks like we might be witnessing the early stages of a potential addiction. We know we could be wrong, but we love you and we are afraid for you. Please help us with our fear, we need your help. Because none of us really knows what an addiction looks like, none of us is qualified to say that it is or it isn't, so we must be free to communicate our thoughts and fears. If you do not see anything wrong with your chemical use and it is 'only a weekend thing' and you are not becoming addicted, well then, it will not trouble you at all if we ask you not to drink alcohol or use any other mind and mood altering chemical for a period of 3 months.

To the none addicted individual, not to drink or use, is never an issue

If this request proves to be an issue of contention for you in any way and you find your mood changing for the worse towards us at this point, that would indicate a desire to protect what looks like a negative behaviour which, at the very least, is damaging family relationships. If it is an addiction in the making, you will develop aggressive defensive thinking towards our concerns and our proposal. If a chemical dependency is under development here, it will manifest itself through an addictive type of thought life and, after committing to not drinking or using for an agreed time span, you will somehow find a rational excuse for picking up the chemical again. So basically, as a family who love you, we are asking this of you: if you are not addicted, do not use. Only you can help us with this.

If the family doctor is available to attend, that would help; but the doctor must arrive last. Set the meeting for 7:30 in the evening, invite the doctor to arrive by 8:15. The object of this exercise is to sabotage any potential addiction in a non-threatening environment with non-judgemental exposure. The presence of a medical professional will instill a sense of empathy within the group and the potential addict may begin to understand that you really want to understand.

Try to keep the following in mind: most addictions are flirted with in bravado, conceived in naiveté, developed in secret and survive on shame and fear within the hearts of people who, by nature, cannot distinguish between good and evil.

If our problematic individual is approached with humility, they may respond in humility. If the way we approach the problem is perceived as accusatory in any way, a power struggle is created, the motives of everyone become twisted and the winning of the point becomes more important than the winning of the person. Do not go into this meeting under the government of media - created fears. If a chemical dependency is under way, please keep in mind that it is only still under construction, it is a future thing. We must not use artillery-like ultimatums or strict punishment based consequences at the table of early negotiation. A kind word dispels wrath. Sit down and chat, open a tin of biscuits and create as relaxed an atmosphere as possible. As soon as the doctor arrives, make the approach. If a chemical dependency is under development, this meeting may not stop it, but I believe if handled correctly, it could at least prove to be a significant contributing factor in shorten its life-span. This meeting will implant a certainty into the user's heart that with respect to any further chemical use, the games are over. We will also open the eyes of the potential addict to an unavoidable awareness of the concerns of the people who love him, sabotaging all future attempts to 'enjoy' recreational drug usage.

CHAPTER SEVEN

ESCALATION

Confirmation that we are looking at a potential addiction will be seen in the response to our relaxing empowerment. If a promise of adherence to our requests is made, we are almost certainly looking at an addiction. The deceptive mind blinds the budding addict from the fact that promises are manipulations. Not only will he make promises, he himself will believe the promises. Further confirmation of an addiction in the making will be that as soon as he does stop for a period of time, he will use the fact that he was able to stop to convince himself that 'he cannot therefore be an addict' and he will then use again. He will judge himself as 'not being alcoholic' whilst he is in a season of not drinking, as opposed to honestly looking at the chaos and pain in his life whilst he is drinking.

Early indications that our recreational user is turning into an abuser will be a slow increase in withdrawal symptoms. There will be unpredictable emotional swings as what was once a fun-loving person starts to display more and more moodiness, and there will often be unnecessary explosions of aggression. Ever so slowly 'users' start to become disinterested in none-using friends, favorite sports, employment and/or studies. The emotional dilemma that the budding-junky suffers from is usually something like this: they isolate because of an increasing sense of loneliness and they are constantly haunted by feelings of shame *and* pride at the same time. It's an emotional and psychological phenomenon.

The only way for the potential addict to make any sense of this conflict in life is to mix with people of a similar condition. Relationships with non-using family members and work colleagues become arduous. A silently cynical character assassin starts to find fault in anyone and everyone who might just be getting on with their life without anywhere near the same amount of chemical consumption. The shroud of deception blinds the addict to the fact that not only is his confidence being eaten away, but what should be a healthy level of Social Anxiety starts to feel overly intense. It, like every other feeling, gets denied and subsequently goes into hibernation where it grows. Depending on the length of the addiction and the types of drugs used, I believe this Social Anxiety can grow into any one of many anti-social mindsets, even paranoia.

Students

There is a very attractive deception abroad that sounds like this: stimulants enable students to study throughout the hours of darkness whilst simultaneously improving their powers of concentration and retention.

A recent client of ours 'achieved' a distinction in her studies. However, she had used stimulants to 'help' her. Following 'graduation' she ended up in therapy and having to contend with the feelings of shame due to her cheating. Her personal development froze and her recreational chemical usage matured into an addiction. Recovery became impossible until she approached the university in question confessed her wrong. Deserving students, her 'friends', who had also studied long and hard, had to settle for second place to a cheat; not the platform upon which to build a career. Her subsequent confession also saved her from finding herself in a career for which, in truth, she was not emotionally equipped. Instead of reaching any height of success, her cheating isolated her from any honest social interaction and increased her chemical abuse.

For this young lady, like millions of other naïve recreational drug users, life slowly deteriorates. Saturday night may have once be the focal point of the week, but as things escalate and we take an aerial view of the week we see another story.

Most of Sunday is spent in bed, drifting in and out of a niggling restlessness, with memory flashes from the previous night. Feelings of guilt and shame sometimes physically move the user as they recall some shameful public behaviour. Irrational fear is never very far from the surface rendering it impossible to lay still for any length of time. If the family has already held the Relaxing Empowerment meeting, it will be in these moments of quiet reflection that the principles of truth will start to germinate. Should the truth be seen and embraced by our user at this point, they can be steered away from the chaos of addiction with an accurate therapeutic intervention. However, because most potential addicts have an ability to intimidate the people who love them, in conjunction with a deceptive and self-righteous attitude of "I will surely not die", the slide usually continues and another life gradually takes over.

Monday mornings become really difficult because of the withdrawal related mood swings. Eye-to-eye contact with loved ones becomes increasingly difficult and there will be a growth in aggressive defensive rationalizations. Users soon stop talking *to* their significant others and start talking *at* them. The 'recreational season' slowly evolves into a regular weekend intake and an inevitable growth in the variety of chemicals being used. There is a tolerance built up in the user and they simply do not get what they used to from (a) their specific drug of choice or (b) the amount they use. They became emotionally constipated and spontaneously dishonest. Within the first year or two, most potential addicts grow out of touch with real feelings and find themselves trapped between feeling of either being extremely high or deeply miserable. Thoughts of stopping are never very far from the abuser's mind, but nothing ever happens with these thoughts.

Potential addicts somehow cling on to a distorted notion that they will clean up at some point. They judge themselves by their ambitions and sadly believe their own promises.

The shift from chemical abuse to chemical dependency will come with the manifestation of symptoms like a rapid decline, even abandonment of personal responsibility around employment and personal hygiene. There will be an increase in aggressive behaviour and lies, family fights will become a daily occurrence, and there will be an all round growth of distrust. It will affect everyone so deeply that they will start to cringe every time the phone or the door bell rings. In-house resentments and hurts thwart any possibility of healthy communication. A line gets crossed where life may never be the same again. I believe everyone involved would benefit from trying to achieve a personal degree of acceptance around the fact that 'life may never be the same again'. Because no one saw the addiction developing within our struggling individual, it therefore has to be said that no one saw how life was actually lacking for them. We must abandon the ideal of trying to get things 'back to how they were'. If you go back to 'how you were' you will once again end up in treatment. We must change forward.

CHAPTER EIGHT

ADDICTION

Chemical users see using as nothing really to worry about. Chemical abusers argue about the right to use. Addicts create arguments to create reasons to use.

The addict will now rigorously add the finishing touches to the denial system around his need for the chemical and his life-controlling desires to use. In many ways he becomes like Gollum in Lord of The Rings protecting *his precious;* he will keep the world out whilst dying of loneliness.

It is a very thin line between recreational chemical use, unpredictable chemical abusage and the powerlessness of chemical dependency, but the differences are huge. No one can pin down exactly where the abuse ended and addiction began, because it is so subtle and each person is different, but one common denominator unfailingly exists within the belief system of those who eventually pass through to an addiction; they each share a desperate cry - 'this was never the plan'.

For most, there comes a realization morning when they simply have to face it - they are no longer using the chemicals; the chemicals are now using them. The pain of facing up to this failure is so intense that the deepest need of the addicted one is to be approached much in the same way as you would if you were going to tell them they had cancer.

Things change drastically now. What used be nothing more than a two-day spree of using and a three-day period of preoccupation, now turns into periodic midnight sobbing sessions and a daily yearning to be understood and to be free. In this condition, addicts are relentlessly haunted by a life-governing urgency for the influence of their desired chemicals. Where once he used to lie awake and think about the using the drug, now he finds himself covered in sweat, gripped by cramps, tossing and turning and scheming for ways to get more of a drug that he has grown to hate, whilst he slowly loses hope of ever 'not using' again.

It used to bring significance and security; now it just chases away nightmares and physical torture. It used to take part of his salary; now he is unemployed and unemployable, everything he touches turns to stolen. He feels bad about himself because of the depths to which he finds himself willing to go in order to pay for the drugs. The worse he feels about himself, the more drugs he needs. Deep down, he knows, 'I'm dying'. There will be daily futile attempts not to use, with heartbreaking relapses, resulting in more failure and more using. In his empty broken heart, he knows, the point of the needle has turned into a barbed hook and during the silent weeping of many early mornings he inwardly vows to get clean 'today'. He has sadness and tears in his eyes yet aggression in his voice. He promises himself and his loved ones 'I will stop' and in a distant part of his darkening imagination he actually believes his own promises. It could be said that he never made a promise that he did not believe. He will make the promises to family and friends and very often somehow manage repeatedly to get them to believe in him. Over and over, he will instill false hope within everyone around him. He sounds so convincing because he actually believes what he is saying. However, as soon as his victims allow themselves to trust him again, seduced into his governing dynamic of deception, once again, he steals from them to buy drugs and the hopes of everyone are once again shattered. Gone are the feelings of invincibility and omniscience. Vanished, too, have the 'sensations' of acceptance from the surrounding members of the identity-less drug culture. He will eventually end up all alone, hooked, and his whole day will revolve around lying, cheating, stealing and using. Shame-driven now, he lives a lonely nocturnal life style flitting from drug den to drug den, from bar to bar, stealing or begging anything from anyone in order to fund the demands of the cursed chemical dependency which has achieved absolute sovereignty over his heart, mind and life. This addictive trap is, in my view, best described by our brethren of Alcoholics Anonymous, in their little blue "12 x 12" when they tell us: 'we were victims of a mental obsession so subtly powerful that no amount of human willpower could break it'[5]. Whether the chemical be alcohol or heroin; the spiritual, physical, psychological and financial decay feels exactly the same. The intensity of the holistic demise is only equalled by the frustration he feels at his pathetic life and his membership of a tribe of a similarly dying people with whom he actually has nothing in common. For the intravenous addict, the needle going in is often excruciatingly painful during this season of deterioration, as he has to sometimes pierce through tender swollenness from yesterday's botched injection attempts. Yes it's painful, but never so painful enough to sustain any thoughts of not injecting. Compensationary measures will include frequently drinking lots of energy drinks and doing lots of press-ups in a pathetic attempt at self-medicating the shattered ego within the dying frame. In reality, when he is alone, he will not be able to escape from the fact that he is slowly but surely fading away, averaging somewhere in the region of three square meals a month. Current users and abusers reading this chapter who now tell themselves, 'I will never get to that state' – have just stepped one step closer to this state.

His internal dialogue is constantly abusive, unnecessarily negative and consistently critical towards himself and towards the world around him. In and of himself, he cannot see any way of halting this destructive and eventually fatal process. He is a member of the 'drug culture' now, where 'time off' is out of the question and there is no such thing as 'Christmas'; it's just another day in torment.

---

5. Twelve Steps and Twelve Traditions, Pocket Edition, A.A. World Services In. Page 22

CHAPTER NINE

THE SELF-FULFILLING PROPHECY

It may be worthwhile mentioning at this point how the phenomenon and power of the self-fulfilling prophecy could be a sublime driving force, or, if handled correctly, could be the gateway to recovery. In 1968 psychologists Rosenthal and Jacobsen found a simple way of testing the power of the self-fulfilling prophecy. They went into an ordinary American school and gave the class a 'special' kind of intelligence test. It was actually an ordinary test and they selected a number of children whose performance in the test was about average. Instead of speaking to the children directly, they allowed the class teacher to 'overhear' a conversation in which they named these average children as the ones who, on the basis of this test, were likely to make special progress in the coming year. When they came back a year later, they found that, sure enough, those children were now near the top of their classes. The teachers had believed that these children would do well and had unconsciously given them special attention and intimate encouragement, improving the self-concept of each child by the application of their own revised 'expectations'[6]. With this in mind, I believe it would be appropriate to bring in a thought for family members. The children in the example above listened to and reacted to the 'silent appraisal' of the supportive teacher. He believed that they were potential leaders of their peers and treated them as such and we can then see that they started to believe; 'hey, maybe I can do this' and their 'self-concept' slowly but surely changed.

Personal experience: I dropped out of school during the end of school examination period. I stuck around just long enough to gain two passes, one in Technical Drawing and one in English Literature. Mr. Murphy

---

6. Book 1 of The Home Learning College (UK) Diploma in Psychology
– www.homelearningcollege.com

was our Technical Drawing teacher; he was the only teacher who ever sat me down and called me 'Colin'. From time to time he would simply place an arm around my shoulders and speak words of support about my efforts. My English teacher, in my eyes, was the sweetest, friendliest teacher on planet earth. I felt safe at their approach and scrutiny and I believed that they believed, so I believed and I passed their subjects.

For those of us struggling with or being directly and negatively affected by an active destructive addiction, I think we would do well to examine the implications of the self fulfilling prophecy. Look at the atmosphere within your own home and see if you can identify any 'silent dynamics' which might have governed the mood within the home and your relationships with each other. Things like fear and suspicion which create a silent desire 'to get them to feel their guilt' so that 'they will start to see things my way'. These are the silent ingredients which have all contributed to the decay thus far. Even when our struggling individual makes an attempt at honesty and staying clean and sober, he still receives the silent message of 'Oh it won't last' and so it does not last. You think you have that attitude because he keeps drinking, but maybe he does not believe he can get sober because you have that attitude.

In order to contribute to the recovery of a struggling loved one, especially he or she who has been away in treatment, whilst they are away we may need to establish how much of the responsibility for these dynamics belongs to them and how much belong to you, or they will resurface when my child returns. My child going away and changing will not change me; only I can take responsibility for that. If, as is common for chemically dependent people, our child has a tendency to become like the people he mixes with, when he or she returns, in order to protect himself, he will have to abandon any thoughts of sharing any struggles with you, because of your resentfully distrustful lens. He then inevitably returns to his governing dynamics of fear and guilt and his internal dialogue will then start to sound something like this; "what's the point of struggling to stay clean? I'm damned if I do and I'm damned if I don't, so I might as well take a drink".

The wide and varied damages caused within an active destructive addiction inevitably implant what psychologists call a 'depressive attribution relational style' within the hearts and minds of everyone involved, including those of the addict. Simply put, this means that because of the hurt created within everyone, it is more 'probable' than 'possible' that attitudes towards an individual coming out of an active destructive addictive life style will be both verbally and silently negative. Even if the individual goes into treatment or prison, if the hurts are left unresolved, no matter how long the individual may be away or no matter how much clean time he or she might achieve, whenever he returns, relational interactions will be governed by the dormant 'individual response to people, places and things which are seen as having the potential to endanger physical or psychological well being'[7] – the clinical definition of; stress. It must also be noted at this point that the returning addict, whether rightly or wrongly, also sees you as a threat to his physical or psychological well being and is also instinctively inclined toward wanting to protect himself. Family support does not come in the form of what we say or don't say; it comes more from within the change in their own attitude resulting from the removal of their own hurts and resentments. All concerned will then benefit from the corresponding belief that; 'only acceptance, truth and grace can get us through this together'. Don't support or judge the struggle from the sidelines, silently join in with your own programme of development.

Relapse is conceived within the addict when, from a platform of his own unresolved anxieties, he picks up on resentments held towards him, and he starts to take responsibility for the hurts inside other people. This is how the guilt of his past life overpowers his right to be on planet earth and he starts to walk on egg shells again.

For an individual returning from a period of therapy, every effort made to apply recovery principles taught in treatment, will be met with one of two equally destructive reactions:

1. An over-enthusiastic response, sounding something like this: "It's great to have you home, you can get back to work now or you can start your studies again, it'll be great to see you back at the office". Within the struggling recovering individual, this response is very often translated into high expectations and whilst it compliments his inner ambitions,

---

7. Ibid – Module 1 Book 2

it actually negates his right to feel insecure and vulnerable – relapse begins.

Or

2. A depressive attributional response, sounding like this: 'I wonder how long it will last this time' or 'we've seen all this before'. This in turn is received by the struggling recovering individual as extremely threatening and deeply unfair – relapse begins.

Solution:

1. Stop hiding from the truth and take ownership of personal contribution

2. Stop waiting for the addict to take responsibility for your condition

3. Stop playing the blame game

Any struggling recovering individual returning from therapy to a former battle ground needs to be attending somewhere in the region of 90 after-care and/or 12 Step Recovery group sessions in 90 days or as close there to as he can. His entire focus of responsibility has to be on getting through the first 90-days without the use of mind and mood altering chemicals. Careers can wait, wives can wait, children can wait and all your hopes and dreams can wait. If a relapse is triggered by 'outside concerns' the struggling recovering individual will very possibly be blind to it until it is too late if distracting agendas take precedence. Some are fortunate enough to get back into treatment; many, sadly, die.

If there are no support groups in the area, residential aftercare is strongly recommended.

CHAPTER TEN

DETERMINATION

By the time we arrive at the determination phase of the active destructive addiction, there will very probably be an accumulation of recovery attempts, relapses, relational collapses and job losses. The driving energy to do something about the situation, therefore, can very often be shame, guilt, loneliness and fear, and an unrelenting impending sense of doom. This persistent haunting very often drives the emotionally crippled addict even further into the Deceptive government of the self-will, sounding something like this: "I got myself into this mess so I **will** get myself out of it." However, in reality, he is only sinking deeper and deeper into a vortex of poisonous perceptions. In his heart and mind he will grow in the belief that the whole world is turning against him, and in his heart mind, he will also believe several lies that they actually should turn against him.

The reason behind dying addicts finding these lies so easy to believe and impossible to shake off is; they are still under the governing dynamics of Deception. This is why I personally believe the Determination phase is conceived within the majority of addicts in a similar fashion as to Siamese twins within the womb of the unsuspecting mother. The individual's Determination is directly attached to and feeds on the Escalation phase: they grow together, and it is going to take intricate surgery to separate them.

The more we use, the louder the inner niggle niggles about not using so much. The louder the inner niggle niggles, the more we resolve to do something about it, but it is always going to be addressed tomorrow. Without realizing it, the inner niggle gets quieter and quieter and the addict slowly but surely drifts away from his conscience.

Detached from conscience, the addict starts to function within another psychological condition called Cognitive Dissonance, an inner tension created by attempting to agree with two contrasting thoughts at the same time. In the Escalation state, using behaviours frequently and blatantly stand in direct contradiction to the struggling individual's hopes and intensions which were in place before the addiction took over. Let's not forget, the now addicted individual 'was only going to experiment with drugs' and was thereafter 'only going to play' with them. However, because an addiction is superior in strength to idealistic ambitions, these intensions regularly shift and change under the arrogance of Determination. They have to in order to accommodate: (a) continued promises and (b) continued chemical usage, and it is inevitably from within the same deceptive spiritual and psychological marshlands which saw the addict gravitate into the addiction, that we now see an uprising of the deadly Determination.

This is where most damage is done - within the struggling addict's belief and internal dialogue. I believe that it is here, during repeated failed recovery attempts, that every depressive attributional message ever sent to the addict throughout his life is now most likely to become true. This is where many addicts fall prey to the fatal self-fulfilling prophecy: 'I was born a junkie, I'll die a junkie and the world will be a better place without me". Now, in his darkest hour, he will lose all hope of ever going free.

Initial recovery attempts are always seasoned with distorted motives, so keep in mind that even at his most desperate, he is still captive to the deceptive spiritual DNA where 'right sounds wrong' and 'wrong sounds right'. By nature, this guy believes that he is ready to do whatever it takes in order to get it right, but in these early stages of attempting to get clean this is more often than not a groundless belief. To him, the concept of "abstinence from mind and mood altering chemicals and the daily application of a spiritually developmental recovery programme"[8] will be too much too soon. He will readily and willingly address the addiction and the various chemicals of his recent usage, but he will unconsciously harbor reservations around other chemicals that he never had problems with.

---

8. This authors definition of 'Recovery'

Subliminally he will be hoping for a future lesser degree of chemical activity. Being chemically dependent, his only way of handling life so far has been down a path of least resistance; and although his desires to get clean are sincere, his awareness of and ability to deal maturely with the pain, trauma and grief in front of him is still at the underdeveloped maturity level of his pre-experimentation days.

Some time ago, when he stood at the gateway of Experimentation, it may well have been that he had never previously experienced anything traumatic or that he never had to learn the life skill of dealing with stress and social anxiety. Maybe every emotional, physical and material need was met by 'loving parents' who never said 'no' to their little sweetums. Alternatively it could be that he came from a background of neglect and rejection, where none of his needs were ever appropriately met by anyone whom he could trust. Either way, the devastating consequences remain the same as do the requirements for getting out of the active destructive cycle of addiction.

Now at the Determination phase, sliding towards a chemically inspired rock bottom, he can in no way know how to recognise the stress he is suffering from nor how to protect himself from the deadly effect of 'not dealing' with it. The child is now truly 'spoiled' (flawed, disfigured, tainted) and he quite rightly 'expects' someone else either to understand his silent struggles and to take the problem away, or for them to point at him in disgust and to mock: 'I told you so', and why wouldn't they?

Most addicts initially voice desires for recovery because they are sick and tired of the consequences of their addiction. They want everyone off their back and for life to return to their perception of what they believe 'normality' is. Looking for safety and freedom, yet still under the deceptive government and now carrying various trauma issues accumulated in the addiction, they expect a life of normality through painless change. Still judging their efforts by their intentions, they get resentful when you do not pay them the respect they feel they 'deserve', especially when they say that they eventually break and claim to want help!

The addict will instinctively deny the truth of what they have become by trying to determine who they think they have to be, when in truth, they were never really encouraged or guided in how to discover and accept who they really are. In our guidance from the Determination phase through to recovery we may eventually move on from this condition. However, sadly, throughout the struggles ahead, many frequently return to it. I have found this Determination condition to be where many addicts die. The more they try - the more they fail - the more they fail - the more it hurts – the more it hurts – the more drugs they take - the more drugs they take - the worse it gets - the worse it gets - the harder they try, the harder they try, the worse it gets, ad-infinitum.

We are near the bottom now, but such is the dogged strength and internal resilience of man, one can spend chaotic years in this condition. Contemporary social ignorance, intolerance and arrogance very often looks at addiction as a weakness. This belief is far from true, and life may have to get just a tad worse before the deadly 'determination' of the self-will can be fractured.

CHAPTER ELEVEN

DESPERATION

Unfortunately and often fatally, not many people get clean from being sick and tired of the consequences of their addiction. Failure after failure within the determination condition eventually gets the addict to what could fairly be described as 'humanity's basement'. Worthlessness and hopelessness become the governing agents of the inner most being and there is nothing but a darkness of soul to look forward to, day after day, night after night. Each waking moment is devoured by desires for oblivion and eventually they reach the place where they become sick and tired of being sick and tired. This depth of desperation creates within our dying individual either a willingness to go to any length to get clean or the desire for suicide, but by the time we arrive at this condition, not many addicts have enough money or credibility to get their hands on enough money for treatment or for enough drug to overdose on. I believe prison suicides are so common from people coming out of an active destructive addiction because whilst they are in prison, they judge themselves by their behaviour in active addiction, leaving confused and heartbroken families behind with no hope of closure; children left parentless and parents left childless, each alternating between blaming themselves and blaming each other.

Each asking why, yet none of them finding any understanding of how their loved one's deterioration was actually the result of a spiritual search for: Connection, Significance and Security.

CHAPTER TWELVE

INTERVENTION

When the time comes for us to undertake an intervention, it is imperative that we make our approach with sensitivity, humility and compassion. The goal of the intervention could be the difference between life and death, not just right and wrong. We must keep in mind that we are heading into a hostile territory governed by hidden dynamics like a broken heart, a shattered ego and a propensity to lie. We must not try to shepherd our children into our perception of what is right for them, because by this stage most of our motives are fear driven and can very easily create further problems. Family members very often try to steer dying loved ones into the spiritual fog of 'their own desires for them'. The goal of our intervention has to be that we set out on a journey with the destination of our loved one eventually asking this question: "What must I do to be saved"? If they are not asking to be saved, we are asking for trouble. Before we look at suggestions for a programme of intervention for this Determination phase, let's just recap asking the question, 'how would one effectively intervene at the primary conditions of the addictions process?'

INTERVENTION OF DECEPTION

Proverbs 22:6 "Train up a child in the way he should go and when he is old he will not depart from it"

Prevention is better than cure. **Proverb 22:6** does not mean if we 'lecture' a child on how we want them to live they will remember it. I believe a far more accurate exegesis of this proverb would be: "we, by the way we live our life in the home, in the way we relationally, practically, verbally and silently guide the children in our care, we exhibit the way life is to be lived, then when they grow they will be unable to avoid repeating that style". Our way of life will carry more of an influence into our children's hearts and minds than our morality and philosophies on life. Since we are told in Scripture that we "all fall short of God's Glory," would it not stand as a living witness to the truth of God if we sat with our children even from infancy, as fellow pilgrims, and communicate the truth of the hopelessness of the fallen nature and it's propensity towards deceptive ways. This way, at an early age, our children will at least be steered towards asking the correct questions - 'what must I do to be saved?' – and The Holy Spirit is then given an opportunity to fulfill His Divine purpose – 'To convict the world of sin and righteousness and the judgement of God' **(John 16:8).**

INTERVENTION OF EXPERIMENTATION

It is extremely difficult to intervene into the life of an individual if they reach a place of wanting to experiment with mind and mood altering chemicals, especially if you yourself use them. If you want to defend your right to use mind and mood alerting chemicals, you must therefore afford the same privilege to others.

If you are setting out with child rearing and/or planning marriage, why not set out as you would want them to carry on and practice the principle of not using mind and mood altering chemicals yourself in your own life?

INTERVENTION OF RECREATION

If Recreational use is underway, it is essential that every misdemeanor carries a consequence. If the using pattern is not exposed at this point, the problem will grow. Having them complete the following 'balance sheets' can be of immense benefit.

BALANCE SHEET

1. Write out ten positive consequences of continued chemical use

2. Write out ten negative consequences of continued chemical use

3. Write out ten positive consequences of abstinence from chemicals

4. Write out ten negative consequences of abstinence from chemicals

The results of the Balance Sheet will uncover one of two conditions:

1. Deceptions resistant denial with an aggressive defensive response – in which case we are probably uncovering an active addiction

2. Humble submission – in which case we are probably witnessing nothing more than naiveté.

Either way, a recommendation to read this book may be a good idea.

INTERVENTION OF ESCALATION

The indignity of random urine testing will serve to (a) expose and confirm signs of an escalation and (b) bring a Determinational mind-set to the surface. Whilst 12-Step literature accurately promotes three key spiritual requirements for recovery: 'Honesty, Open-mindedness and Willingness'[9] - when dealing with individuals using mind and mood altering chemicals, we must stay vigilant because the heart of what could be a developing addict will not necessarily manifest dishonesty, closed-mindedness and unwillingness. These destructive attributes are inevitable to some degree because of the nature to:

1. Attempt to cover up the damage
   – Genesis 3:7

2. Attempt to hide from the truth
   – Genesis 3:8

3. Attempt to avoid personal responsibility
   – Genesis 3:10

4. Attempt to play the blame game
   – Genesis 3:12

---

9. Alcoholics Anonymous 12 Step Preamble

However it must also be remembered that very often a developing addict will use honesty as a smoke screen to protect their chemical usage. Humility is the only genuine response if we are to stop the rot at the escalation state.

Therefore, if we attempt an Intervention of an Escalation we need to be watching for 'an attitude of indifference or intolerance towards spiritual principles'[10], but not just in the developing addict. I have lost count of the number of Christian parents with whom we have worked who dismiss the principle of looking towards the 12 Step recovery communities for guidance for their offending child. "We believe that Jesus Christ is the only way", they cry, and they frequently then refer back to various testimonies of people whom they have never met, who once made claims of healing miracles, that they have never had the opportunity to test. They then therefore insist that Church involvement, and in many cases even going to Bible College, is all that is needed.

In my experience, recovery from active destructive addiction never fell out of the skies. If Jesus Christ causes a heart to be regenerated by the power of His Holy Spirit, He sets that heart free and converts the desires, but He only sets it free to start learning how to take responsibility for its own growth and its new desires. He does not re-create the finished article. The removal of the compulsion to use mind and mood altering chemicals is an awesome miracle, but it is only the tip of a ministerial, developmental mountain of need. 12 Step recovery veterans, in my opinion, know more about the workings of the destructive and deceptive dynamics of addictions than most Christians know about God and the call to 'walk in the light as He is in the light' (1 John 1:7). Unless believers in The God and Father of The Lord Jesus Christ are willing to become open-minded enough to humble themselves to the truth of the fact that we need to adopt some of what the world is practising, we become vulnerable to hypocrisy, and two wrongs never made anything right. Two wrongs simply make things too wrong.

As we intervene at escalation, we actually declare war on the powerful and deadly deceptive influences of the chemical which will have developed a corresponding power of mind and heart to deceive, and there will almost certainly need to be a supervised period of residential care during the detoxification period until we can see: (a) a willingness

---

10. Ibid

to undertake the previously mentioned attendance of 90 meetings in 90 days with an appropriate 12-step recovery group; (b) a desire to continue a relationship with them thereafter; (c) fruit of change.

If The Lord Jesus Christ has truly liberated this individual's heart, we will not be able to stop them from joining a Church. If, however, we see no desire to join a Church or to take up regular fellowship with other Christians, we are almost certainly witnessing either (a) a victim of religious abuse or (b) a morality shift, something we often see born in a mortality check. Many people stop smoking after being diagnosed with cancer. That's a morality shift born in a mortality check. The problem with the addict is, as soon as the devastating consequences are removed, if an addiction has not been exposed and addressed, it will resurface.

INTERVENTION PROCEDURE

All too often we get distraught family members ringing us or emailing us with the same question: "Is there anything I can do to stop this madness"?

The addict or alcoholic in the family is slowly dying in front of them, but all attempts at reasoning have ended in outbursts of defensive aggression and pleas of innocence from the guilty one, leaving feelings of guilt within the innocent ones.

Family members are left to suffer in silence, damned if they do mention the addiction, damned if they don't. Right sounds wrong and wrong sounds right.

There is a very common misconception that an addict will never get clean until they reach rock bottom. I am inclined to disagree, believing rock bottom can actually be determined by the level of willingness on the part of the addict, and their victims, simply to stop digging.

A common and damaging dynamic within the families of offending addicts is to quietly want some form of revenge or justice for the hurts they have received. If this dynamic comes into play at the intervention, detrimental choices can easily be made. The longer the family members have suffered, the more prone they can be towards wanting 'the addict' broken down and rehabilitated. However, we must remember, our loved one is in there somewhere. It is not the addict which needs to be broken down, it is the deceptive dynamics of the addiction which need to be recognized, exposed and empathetically dismantled. It is the thinking, the motives, and the attitudes that need to be identified and exposed, yet without condemnatory or condescending feedback.

On the one hand there will be an essential need for painfully graphic imagery of what the addiction looks like and feels like through the eyes of and the heart of the victims, whilst simultaneously abstaining from accusatory terminologies. The offending addict needs to know that he is not under attack, but that the addiction is. Once all the dots are accurately connected and the offending addict starts to see a high definition picture of the effects of his life on the world around him, he will then possibly start to feel safe enough to begin to feel regret, remorse and possibly repentance. Only then will his allegiance to the chemical and its corresponding culture be fractured and we can then start to re-capture the wayward child.

Allow me two quotes from hard-chore, long-term addicts who went the course of this approach:

"I came to treatment for one month only. That was the agreement and that was my intention (Determination). I had been through seven other rehab attempts and I could not see what another one could teach me. However, the treatment I received was totally different. I suddenly found my spirituality being addressed and it just felt so refreshing. All the other rehabs either Bible bashed me or told me to establish my own spirituality. I needed to know what my needs were, but I did not know what questions to ask. I eventually stayed for 3-months and then came back as a volunteer to work and study. Slowly, the truth of my need to know God personally dawned on me".

Another guy said, "I can now see that my addiction needed a personal, spiritual touch, rather than the professional, intellectual approach. With all the professionals I was sent to, the common sense factor of my spiritual needs was overlooked".

Intervention must gently but firmly disempower the addict, in order to re-empower the family and for them to reclaim their home. Until now the addict has dictated the mood of the home and most family members are exhausted from the emotional stress placed upon them.

The time has come for action, not revenge. Call a meeting in the home. Let the addict know that there is going to be a meeting, but do not include them. Let the addict know who is attending the meeting, but do not tell them anything else.

The Biblical Link to Addiction and Recovery would like to suggest the following procedure of intervention.

STEP ONE

Find a reputable, affordable rehab to which you would like to send the offending addict. Approach the rehab and inform them of your intervention intentions and secure a bed-space for the day of Intervention.

STEP TWO

1. **Make a list of <u>suspected law infringements</u>: jewelry items missing, cell phones missing, furniture items missing, car used without permission, verbal threats inflicted.**

2. **Make a list of physical health infringements: Erratic eating patterns, weight loss, lack of personal hygiene, lack of respectful dress code.**

3. **Make a list of moral infringements: Bad language within the home, aggressive behaviour within the home, intimidation of parents and siblings, persistent breaking of basic in-house boundaries.**

List as many infringements as possible under each of the three headings onto a computer print-out document and have each one witnessed and signed by several family members.

STEP THREE

Arrange a meeting at a neutral venue with Internet access. As far as is possible invite:

1. **Two or three family members**

2. **Family doctor**

3. **One or two police officers**

4. **A Pastor or other religious leader from the community**

5. **Two members of the local 12 Step Recovery community**

6. **The offending addict**

Invite each family member to speak of their fears and hurts

Invite one of the police officers to read out the Infringement Indictments

Invite the doctor to voice an assessment

Invite the 12 Step Recovery representatives to share some of their experience

Designate the primary family member then to read out a statement of ultimatum

ULTIMATUM

"Either receive immediate therapeutic help for this addiction at a reputable rehab of our choice today, or face the only alternatives open to us: (a) a section 21 order for 12-months to a state rehab or (b) an arrest for one or all of the afore mentioned indictments and eviction from residence at this and/or any other family home.

Invite the offending addict to view the reputable, affordable rehab website, and then to decide. If they agree to receive therapy, don't be fooled. The addict only has one thing on mind at this point: how to get through this chaos via the path of least resistance. Have bags packed with immediate necessities and a car full of petrol, but please try to allow the addict's necessary process of grief to run its course. If the doctor could have an appropriate form of medication to dispense at this meeting, it will show the offending addict that everyone concerned, cares. I would anticipate that eight out of ten addicts will storm out at this point. Let them go. They need a hit, allow it. If you have never suffered from a chemical dependency you can in no way imagine the anguish involved at this time for this guy. I can testify; I felt a deeper sense of sadness and loss when I lost access to heroin than I did when I witnessed the death of my mother. The Intervention Procedure will have a phenomenal impact on the addict and his drug using days will be dramatically cut short by it. If he storms out of the intervention meeting, it will be to use, 'one last time'. He may not be able to handle the thought of 'suddenly losing the choice to use'. However, the very next time he uses, he will cease to enjoy the influence of the chemical. Leave them alone, they will come home, wagging their tails behind them.

Once the addicted individual is removed from the drug and the corresponding culture, there will be a week to ten day period of intense physical and emotional detoxification and trauma, during which the addict must be handled with kid gloves and treated with suitable medication and sensitivity as he fights his way through psychological vulnerability.

CHAPTER THIRTEEN

THE ROAD TO DISCOVERY

Deflection

Once the detoxification period starts to subside and the struggling individual starts to emerge, there will be a distortion of motives and desires. There will be a desire for wrong to be right and right to be wrong. Secret internal dialogue will dictate which way the next few days will pan out if it is not exposed. Most 'wanna-be-clean' individuals emerge from their detox and instantly start to believe that 'everything is better now that I feel better'. Whilst they are feeling better than they have felt in months and whilst they are feeling safe, they simultaneously look back with resolve and forward with ideals: "I am never going back there, I've learned my lesson now, I'll show everyone". However, I have come to believe that the one person on earth about whom the addict knows the least, is the addict himself. He believes many things about himself which are in fact not true and there is going to be an inevitable period of grief. Grief over losing the chemicals to which he has grown fully dependent, grief over not turning out to be the person he thought he was, grief at who he has become and a grief over the damages done in the addiction. Whilst it sounds obvious to say that a lot of what he is going to have to face up to is going to be painful, it might not be so obvious either to the emerging individual or to the people around him how his lengthy chemical dependency has disabled him from the natural ability to handle pain. Survival in the addiction culture demands that each of its members adopt various defense mechanisms and coping skills and it will be these skills on which the struggling to recover individual will instinctively fall back.

Recommended reading for further insights into the dynamics of the addiction culture is Pathways[11]

The Road to Recovery is never an event; it is invariably only ever discovered within the process of struggle. Recovery does not begin in the past or in the future; it has to be worked out in the here and now, but because of our nature to avoid pain, it has to begin with a humble prayer and a sincere request for: (a) courage to come out of hiding from the truth, (b) the desire to start taking personal responsibility and (c) the willingness to abandon the search for someone to blame. Anything else is what The Biblical Link to Addiction and Recovery calls a deflection. Deflections come in various styles and with a multitude of manipulative techniques, but they are not wrong; they are abnormal behaviours for normal people powerlessly trapped in an unmanageable lifestyle. We disqualify ourselves from helping as soon as our own secret internal dialogue starts to sound like this: 'Oh this poor wretch, he really needs my help'. The emerging individual in our care has to undergo a whole programme of un-learning before he can be introduced to the struggles of early recovery.

Our struggling individual cannot relapse at this stage of the journey because they have to be clean in order to relapse. They are only chemical free at this early stage. Chemical free is only chemical free, it does not equate to clean. Taking personal responsibility for the truth of the ugliness of the problem whilst chemical free is that which makes a person clean. Until they start that process, they can have no way of knowing the quality of peace of heart and mind that recovery can bring. They cannot possibly yet comprehend the depth of spiritual, psychological and emotional stability available to them if they will only get honest. Recovery promises stability enough to enable even the worst of cases to survive the rigors of the blistering heat of a brutal wilderness without even craving a drink. He can in no way yet comprehend how he could ever live a life free from the destructive bondages of the self, nor enjoy the weirdest of desires of living a life for the blessing and development of the people around him and for the glory of a God who loves him.

---

11. White William L. 1996. Pathways. Hazelden. Center City Minnesota. ISBN 1-56838-123-9

At this stage of emergence, addicts believe that all they have to do to be clean is to avoid taking drugs.

Now we find ourselves with a very vulnerable individual whose entire history speaks of an inability to face life on life's terms. As was previously mentioned, most addicts actually believe someone else should sort out the problem for them. Right up until arriving in treatment, most offending addicts have never been chemically free long enough to learn how handle the pressures of life in an appropriate manner. They tend to swing to extremes and believe that they are now expected to face up to the years of chaos and destruction, by themselves, all at once.

Remember, many distorted expectations have been implanted and will continue to play a role during this initial window of therapy. Verbally and/or silently, expectant family members who do not understand the deceptive dynamics of an addiction desperately want their loved one back. Our goal must not be to 'get the loved one back'; we must never settle for anything less than to see a new person emerge by going forward, whatever that means or whatever it entails.

Keep it real. Addicts have a knee-jerk reaction of dishonesty towards the first perception of a threat. His whole being is programmed to protect (a) himself and (b) the addiction, from any form of exposure; and the stress of now being removed from that chemical is immense. They become emotionally, spiritually and psychologically vulnerable all at once, and their perception is that the pain of getting into recovery has to be more intense than the pain of going back into addiction. Deflection is not a bad thing; it is a necessary part of the growth process which, to the addict, feels like his only means of immediate survival. If the entire severity of the addiction hit home all at once, I believe we would see more suicides that we already do. Denial is a healthy coping mechanism which enables addicts to come to terms with the truth at a pace that is manageable for them. Because the addict cannot possibly understand what is taking place, nor fully grasp the size of what he has to face up to, he naturally starts to find reasons to be somewhere else or to become overly involved in someone else's issues.

Remember that we somehow have to enter the addict's psychological and emotional carnage, everything he has been trying to deny and hide. As soon as they even perceive that they are not being understood, we will lose them. In fact the addictive inclination within them is actually to set out and go 'looking' to be misunderstood so that he can use again. This, I believe, is where only the long-term clean and established ex-addicts can earn the right to speak into the chaos of the emerging manipulative individual.

Our long term goal for this individual is for them to achieve freedom from the bondages of chemical dependency and for them simply to take up life within the 'normal' boundaries of their emotional and intellectual capabilities. If we keep in mind how man is actually supposed to function: 'Intellect over Emotion', and consider how we now find ourselves with a person totally out of touch with his emotions, we find the primary area of deflection: the battlefield of the mind. Our immediate concern has to be that we do not make right sound wrong. Their belief is: 'I cannot do this". We must support them in that belief because it is true, they can't. Once we get them to this belief we must anchor them there. I have frequently seen this mind-set to be the pre-development phase of many a recovery process. Our client has been removed from his chemical and the destructive culture; all he is looking for at this point is an understanding mentor who can offer him a simple and sensitive explanation about the emotional chaos within him right at this moment. Reassurance is increased further when in the midst of the confusions we simply sit with them and explain, 'this chaos is a perfectly normal reaction for someone coming out of a battle zone'. Somehow we have to get this person to understand that we understand, because that's the only time he will start to feel safe enough to go forward without deflection.

In an article in the Jewish World Review, Rabbi Abraham J. Twerski was once as quoted as saying: 'all of my writings revolve around Numbers 13:33 "There we saw giants and we were like grasshoppers in our own sight and so we were in their sight". Rabbi Twerski was trying to answer this question; 'how can we know factual reality when our emotions distort our perceptions'? From the verse in Numbers he concluded that the way we feel about ourselves is how we think others perceive us. The context of the text is that of spies being sent to survey the land of God's promise (Recovery). They saw giants in the land and responded with a fearful assessment of themselves and a twisted perception of the giant's opinion of them (Relapse). For addicts coming out of an active destructive addiction, the picture is exactly the same. They arrive in treatment, and with the removal of the chemicals, the road to recovery starts to look very scary. Planet earth starts to look like it is occupied by giants who all look extremely grown up and mature. Within the struggling individual there is a deep sense of shame and failure; and he transfers on to the world around him the way he feels about himself by telling himself 'they don't believe I can do this'.

Progress will only be made when those involved can distinguish between good and evil, who are strong enough to uphold painful truth and when they themselves can display a life of personal growth and responsibility.

Understanding brings empowerment, but only change brings change.

If the addiction is addressed from a purely professional stance, it becomes impersonal and the addict will eventually disappear into a maze of deflections. If they instinctively resort to skills developed within the addiction culture, they will stay in addiction. If the addiction is addressed from a purely personal stance, a potentially manipulative individual will see this as a weakness and a very subtle contempt will creep in and the addictive mindset will soon be in control of the transition process.

The emerging individual needs to be treated with a professionally personal touch, with nothing in mind but desires for their freedom. Do not make 'rehabilitation' the focus. Rehabilitation has to be the fruit of freedom. At some point in this early struggle, their perception of the pain ahead will overwhelm them and in their mind they will clock-out ('emotion over intellect'). They will start to say 'yes' when they mean 'no' and 'no' when they mean 'yes', and without a skilled eye at this point, our addict will go below radar, the treatment will go back under the control of the (deceived) addict and a return to the chemicals is inevitable.

CHAPTER FOURTEEN

Relapse

A return to the chemical is not, in my view, a relapse. A return to the chemical is, in my view, a consequence of a relapse. Picking up the mind and mood altering drug is the penultimate act of a relapse, with prison, death or readmission into treatment being the ultimate end.

There are wide and varied ingredients and reasons that make up a relapse which lead back to chemical dependency and this, I believe, is where the Church needs the guidance of our brothers and sisters of the fellowships of Alcoholics and Narcotics Anonymous. Most of their 12 Step Recovery literature contains attitude and behavioral identification sections that we can all learn from like the following:

Attitudes for Relapse

Omnipotence: Listening and learning stops.

Cockiness: A little bit of information is a very dangerous thing.

Expectations: Real and/or perceived expectations.

Convenient Amnesia: Drifting back into ex-peer groups.

The Death of Daily Disciplines: Personal quiet time is always the first to go.

Little Dishonesties: A pattern of unnecessary little lies sets the wheels in motion.

Argumentative: Tiny issues quickly escalate to boiling point.

Complacency: Addiction is no longer feared, and everything is going well.

Reasons for Relapse

Resentments: The biggest stumbling blocks to recovery.

Negative Emotions: Not knowing how to handle negative emotions positively.

Positive Emotions: Not knowing how to handle positive emotions maturely or responsibly.

Social Pressure: Expecting using friends to respect their recovery.

Relationship conflicts: Many relapses are born within resentment-based relationships.

Testing control: Recovery often convinces people they can now control using or drinking.

Social Stress: Participation in life's mundane functions can be a trial.

Conditioned Reactions: Public lavatories can trigger cravings, it was where we used.

Impatience: I don't want to wait ten years to be ten years clean, I want it today.

At the Intervention and Deflection phases, we must expect any and all of the above dynamics to play a part in the day to day treatment of the addiction. Stay focused, keep the main thing the main thing and focus on the addiction. The more of these attitudes we expose, the less they use them, and the more reasons we dismantle, the higher the likelihood there will be of a new person emerging. Good therapy will not prevent a relapse; good therapy will only empower the stumbling individual and disempower the addiction when a relapse occurs and therefore shorten the life-span of any subsequent active addiction. A relapse will die as soon as there is a return to the truth and personal responsibility is once again embraced.

CHAPTER FIFTEEN

SUBMISSION

The longer the addiction has been active, the stronger the possibility that there will be underlying issues of things such as suicide attempts, incest, rape, incestual rape and even murders, past, recent and/or sometimes intended. What we have is an emotional mine-field.

One would think that a condition of submission would be the natural fruit of decades of chaos and surrounding heartache. Alas, not so. Submission is totally unnatural for fallen people and excruciatingly painful for survivors of the drug culture, because it implies accepting that which feels like 'less-than-failure'.

Submission is very easily misunderstood by both the addict and the carers around them, because it is not just a case of submission *out of* addiction. That's the easy part. Problems start when the time comes for submission *into* reality. Letting go of the addiction sounds like a great idea, right up until we come face to face with the perceived pain of the alternative. This next season is going to need strong hearts and trained eyes in the art of recognizing the difference between right and wrong. The consequences of inappropriately treated addictions are a slow and miserable death. The alcoholic takes a particularly long time to die. Most junkies are dead before they get to the age of 45.

No matter how long and how painful the dark years have been, we are dealing with a very strange personality in the addict and it is this particular condition of Submission that we will regularly have to revisit in the coming battles, even when things are going well. If we can remain tapped into an attitude of Submission, it will become a place of frequent refuge and an oasis during the deserts and droughts of early recovery, with many victories being won in surrender. Any heart in the condition of submission is initially going to feel on the brink of hopelessness and panic. Beware co-dependent feedback.

Flattery at this point - "you can do this, you are worth it, and you are able" - as positive as it might sound (to the speaker), can actually come across as patronizing and detrimental (to the listener). When addicts in this condition arrive for treatment, they first have to be reassured that their feelings are actually right – they are hopeless and they cannot do it. Because most carers feel attached to their struggling addict or alcoholic by this stage, they tend to forget that the addict is actually unable to feel the same level of attachment in return. Before they are emotionally or psychologically able to form healthy – recovery focused – attachments, they are going to need to learn the difference between safe and unsafe people. We regularly treat addicts with extreme trust deficits, yet they start to relax within hours of arriving in our care. I believe this to be because we instantly and silently offer a new line of understanding and direction. Most addicts only feel directionless, because they do not understand exactly where they are! They have thus far been (incorrectly) led to believe that they have to get into recovery from their addiction and that they can achieve this in rehab (fine sounding philosophy). Not so. Indeed this is an impossible task. They first have to be introduced to an accurate programme of individual discovery. The road ahead has to be understandable and achievable from within each individual's confused state of failure. The object of the initial exercise is therefore to 'hook' them with hope. They have to know that a programme of recovery will not be too much for them either to understand or achieve and this is where we bring in the following simple conditional definitions:

Active Addiction = Doing the wrong things for the wrong reasons

Personal Discovery = How do I add to the problem?

Early Recovery = Struggling to do the right things for the right reasons

Mature Recovery = Struggling to do the wrong thing for any reason

Primary Relapse Signs = Doing the right things for the wrong reasons

Inevitably we see a spark of Hope born within the depths of the hitherto dark eyes of our dying clients when they start to see that there may just be a possibility of recovery for them. Not counterfeit, not too soon, not too demanding, genuine hope and freedom, and, as Oswald Chambers once observed: where Hope is Faith is born. What I would add is: let us be vigilant that where hope is born, submission does not die. The pain ahead is too high to get over, too wide to go around and too deep to go under; we simply have to go through it. The key to longevity is keeping the person in touch with two things:

1. The pain of his using 2. The hope of his future

If the reality of the painful condition of what lies behind remains fresh and more intense than the imaginary pain of going forward, we will continue in the direction of the solution. However, as soon as the pain of active addiction gets somehow forgotten, a relapse is conceived.

I make this point now, because in order to continue in the direction of the solution, we are going to have to apply the following Biblical principle . . .

Lamentations 3:40 "Let us examine our ways and test them, and let us return to The Lord".

The Hebrew meaning in the words used here, 'examine our ways', do much more than merely offer a good idea; they invite those who would want to follow God's Word to 'penetrate, search and examine intimately the course of actions within their life'. Within the depths of this verse we are given a picture of a returning exiled pilgrim, heavy laden with accumulated baggage too heavy for him to carry alone. The implication is that there is a need for a return to a starting point due to having lost his way and accepting his need to start again.

We are not invited to undertake self-examination and to return to The Lord with ideas of our own as to how to do it better next time. That would be insane – to repeat the same mistake expecting a different result. The self examination has to result in concession of inner brokenness and the inability to stand before God with anything of ourselves to boast about. A searching fearless moral inventory of our ways must surely spawn, as it did with Solomon, the writer of the third Proverb, a cry of contrition before God.

The Bible shows how King David had 'the Spirit of The Lord upon him' since he was a young boy. In 1 Samuel 16:13 we are shown how God singled him out and set him apart for Ordination. The Bible places immense seriousness on Ordination. It was something so serious that Jesus Himself spent a whole night praying about it before Ordaining His Apostles (Luke 6:12-13). However, despite coming from a God-ordained family and God-fearing cultural background, I believe it is only fair to say that Solomon, clearly having many reasons to cry in contrition before God, did so because he had an inner awareness that God was approachable.

A recent intake into our addiction treatment facility in South Africa, a highly educated middle class English client, was asked about his Bible knowledge and of who Jesus was. After much thought and a shrug of his shoulders his response was, "didn't they kill Him and put a stone on Him"?

This is the same uneducated world-view which we have frequently witnessed, aggressively and passionately declaring 'I do not believe in God'. I would argue that they, like me, do not suffer from 'unbelief' in God; they are starved of an accurate and understandable explanation about God and they are consequently left spiritually dependent.

What we see today, therefore, is an increasing number of chemically dependent individuals who are spiritually under-developed. If they are removed from the chemicals they are only offered a man-ward and god-less society, within which they remain at the mercy of many self-ordained clinicians, too many of whom feed their own egos by clinically defining people who are actually made in the image of God. Personal destructive self-talk within chemically dependent people naturally serves to confirm anything that might even remotely sound like a 'low self esteem' diagnosis and immense levels of hope are ploughed into counsellors.

Whilst most addicts feel that they should be punished because of their destructive life styles, the concept of God always stirs hostility, because the punishment they seek is trivial compared to the concept they have about God's wrath. Tears have a beautiful way of dissolving this denial and twisted belief. We have no option but to go into a season of sadness, regret and deep remorse. We have to meet with every failure, every hurt and every lost dream and examine the exact nature of our wrongs. Counsellors have to be fully established in who they are at this point, because it is going to be extremely emotional. Our aim is to steer the immerging individual to the very precipice of hopelessness, because as many an old AA member will have testified: "for many a dying alcoholic, they could not see that God was all they needed until God was all they had".

CHAPTER SIXTEEN

THE BIBLICAL LINK TO RECOVERY

Reflection

This is where the leaders 'from darkness to light' must continually strive in prayer to understand Divine standards of wrong from right. For every accurate exposure of a deflection there is going to be a visible discomfort and emotional reaction of anger. If there is any personal insecurity within the recovery facilitator at this phase, this is where it will be exposed and motives can very easily become twisted. The addictive mindset and behaviour will very often be to convey silently a message to the counselor that they are losing respect for and starting to drift away from them. They are creating an atmosphere where the counseling has 'obviously failed' and a return to the chemicals therefore inevitable. Remember the goal, 'to disturb the comfortable with the truth of God so that we can comfort the disturbed with the Love of God'. If co-dependency (all men thinking well of me) becomes a driving motivation during these times of disturbance, the best that our dying friend can rely on is our 'Christianity'. God forbid. The only answer is the truth as God sees it. Handled correctly, it will always take us back to submission. Anger (a sign of life) is prerequisite to a healthy season of reflection. It is the first sign of coming out of denial. Rarely can a person be in denial of a truth and be angry about it at the same time. If we want to go forward, we first have to establish our exact location. If we are to introduce the addict to the root nature of their addiction and the failing consequences of self-medicating, our explanation has to be so real that it is self-explanatory. If we are to work in harmony with the addicted individual toward a goal of killing the addiction, it is essential that we kill it at its root source. In order to accomplish that, it is therefore of primary importance that all parties agree that the addiction problem goes deeper than that of it being a disease or a moral deficiency. Our addicted individual needs to recognise and accept that he is dying from neglect of his spiritual, emotional and psychological needs. His chemical dependency having become a fatal substitute for:

1. Spiritual Identity
2. Individual Significance
3. Social Security

Wherein he has to:

1. Mix with miss-fits in order to fit in
2. Behave unacceptably in pursuit of acceptance
3. Establish an identity from people who have no identity

These are the unfortunate realities from which most addicts are dying and they inevitably bring a dawning of sadness and a state of spiritual bewilderment. The reflection phase introduces them to the truth of the hopelessness of their condition. Instinctively they deflect back into a state of self determination with a need to control their immediate circumstances because of what feels like a life and death situation before them. Guilt, shame, fear and failure blind them from seeing the key to their freedom and they tell lies in order to avoid judgment. The truth of man is looking for the grace of God.

We sit with the addicts and slowly take the considerations of their hearts back into the reality of their addictions, remembering that their instinctive reaction will be to follow the theologically established, spiritually genetic behavioral blueprint:

1. Hiding from the Truth
2. Avoiding Personal Responsibility
3. Playing the Blame Game

Our job is to sabotage all deflections by uncompromisingly steering them back to a detailed picture of their addiction. We have to keep the chemically saturated past alive at the same time as pointing to a chemical-free future. In order to accomplish this most effectively, we reflect through each significant area of life, asking for the following outline of reflection to be followed:

In no less than 100 words write out ten graphically specific examples of:

What happened? – (Get them to paint, in writing, graphic pictures of their behaviour). Who was involved? How did your behaviour affect them and their family? How did your behaviour affect you and your family? How did they and their family feel toward you then and now? How did you and your family feel toward you then and now? Would you repeat this behaviour outside of addiction? How do you feel now?

When sharing, if there are no signs of depression – sit silently until they arrive. Our reflections must bring events back to life until the struggling individual starts to see the faces and the emotional damages done to the victims of the active addiction, The conscience has to be unfrozen and disturbed before it can start to seek to be forgiven.

CHAPTER SEVENTEEN

DEPRESSION

We are about to enter into the loss, the grief, the shame, the failure, the hurts and the shattered relationships of the addict's carnage. We are going to find all kinds of unmentionables. Keep in mind that even though much of the addictions consequences are going to be bad enough in and of themselves, to the emerging individual, they are either going to be severely exaggerated or grossly minimized.

I therefore believe it essential that emerging individuals must be in a safe, therapeutic environment in order to get from an active addiction into the discovery process.

One needs to be able to identify and arrest deflections as soon as they are spotted and to be equipped with the ability to steer the deflector back to an attitude of submission before you try to joining the reflection and the depression.

We lead them, we do not follow. Contextualized self-disclosure at this point is a major key to progress. We could be dealing with a person who sold himself in gay porn movies or prostituted his wife for money to buy the drugs, or even beat his Mom in blame.

Statements such as: "I went through the same sort of thing" or "a similar thing happened to me a few years ago" always help, followed by explicit details of resolved personal emotional turmoil. I regularly then make the following statement, 'If I can get through it, anyone can'.

For the more serious sets of circumstances, I have found an inspiring line of approach to be something along these lines: "I hear you, and I am not going to insult your intelligence, it must be unbelievably painful. I had issues in my life that took the first several years of my recovery to work through. But I have to be honest, the pain of dealing with these issues proved to be much less than the pain of trying to hide from them".

Keep him out of hiding. Keep him in the truth. Allow him to get depressed. If and when the broken start to sob at this point, many people want to reach out and touch them to comfort them. This has to be avoided. Too often the one wanting to 'reach out' is reaching out because of a reaction to their feelings of sadness.

Press on.

Do not maximize, patronize or minimize.

Life was hell and people got seriously hurt. Face it and embrace it.

Just love the guy, even weep with him if need be, but do not try to stop his tears. This is why any addictions counselor who comes out of the addiction culture has to be established in their own recovery. They have to be in touch with their feelings and mature enough to express appropriately them without 'over responsibility'.

This is where I feel we as Christian counsellors must differ. Where the secular world will tell its counsellors, "Stay detached, keep it professional", I believe myself safe enough to get attached and personal without over-involvement, although this was something I learned through bitter experience.

I have found one of the most damaging dynamics within a man has been facing up to the fact that he sold himself in gay sex for drugs. If the guy is gay then this practice will be par for the course. However, I have found many men who were not gay to have done this and the shame is soul-destroying. These devastating patterns of behaviour take place (a) in the hunt for drug money and (b) in the hunt for identity.

Any identity is better than identity-less-ness.

During the treatment of an addiction, whenever someone has shared and exposed depth of shame like the examples above, I always find it takes us forward if, after the session is closed, I simply go about my day. Two or three hours later, I will go back to my struggling friend and just sit with him, maybe take him a cup of tea and quietly tell him how privileged I feel that he saw me trustworthy enough to take such depth of risk in sharing with me. I then return the compliment and take the risk of telling him that I feel a sense of "admiration" and "closeness" and "safety" with him since he shared with me. Over the days that follow, we invariably see a dawning of freedom within the heart and eyes of our client.

Grace promoting truth.

At this early stage though, even 'honest disclosure' can be a smoke screen and a build up to deflection, so during all emotional vulnerability you must stay vigilant.

Telling the truth is not always honest. Very often we see people getting honest because 'honesty is the best policy'. True is the cliché that says 'as soon as you get honest for that reason, you are dishonest'.

In addiction we find people tell us some truth about themselves so that they can then walk out on us. They set themselves up for rejection. Love and a non-judgmental approach can often be the attracting factor in bringing them back on track. They may still deflect, but we stay true. Least ways then, if we do lose them, their lasting memory of us as they re-enter the darkness of addiction's dungeon will be how we displayed Grace and Truth. Many times we have received people back into our care who experienced this 'haunting memory' and it proved to be the saving trigger that brought them back to us when their relapse eventually raped them. For many it would appear that the last strands of resistance are cut by a relapse and it is only then that our message really starts to shine through for them.

CHAPTER EIGHTEEN

ILLUMINATION

This, in my view, is by far the most vulnerable, misunderstood and disrespected condition with which I have worked in many years of addiction counseling. I personally believe that this is where all relapses are born, and this, I believe, is why ...

The process from addiction to recovery usually follows a five-step state of heart:

- Denial – There is no problem, what is everyone worried about?

- Anger – Why can't people just leave me alone?

- Bargaining – Ok, so there is a problem, but it's not that bad is it?

- Depression – I am addicted, I am powerless, I am hopeless

- Acceptance – Ok, let's get this sorted out once and for all

By the time people get to treatment they are usually hovering somewhere between Anger and Depression. The goal is to get them to an attitude of acceptance about the severity of the problem and the extent of their responsibility. Each of the five conditions mentioned above has characteristics unique to itself. Before we can get people to the acceptance, we have to steer them through the bargaining and the depression. We regularly find that it is during the bargaining and depression seasons that our clients get the majority of their 'light-bulb' moments about the nature of their condition. We often hear our clients making the following statement: "Oh, now I understand"- and right there, right at that point, we see the beginning of the end of their discovery programme. They, being prone to extremes, receive one or two "A-Ha" moments during a lecture or a group session and it's as if they start to believe that they have gained a 'total understand' of their condition and they start to then lean on their own understanding. Our 'understanding' therefore is much more than a word and carries much more energy than an intellectual growth spurt. When we gain a new understanding of something, the actual 'inclinations and intentions of the heart' are simultaneously affected. Receiving a new understanding within this context can genuinely feel like a 'spiritual awakening', and when it happens it silently ignites a sincerity to live by the newly understood principles of recovery. Clients then start to believe that they have had a spiritual awakening and that they now have enough information to stay clean.

In a Biblical sense what we have experienced here is 'false light' - another form of counterfeit spirituality which can only ever really produce good intentions. Experience has taught us much, but nothing more than every alcoholic to pass through our doors was filled with 'good intensions'.

During treatment, when clients are seen to be experiencing what we call IOU's (Illuminations of Understanding), we bring in a Bible study on why The Apostle John said in 1 John 2:8 – 'the darkness is passing and the True Light is already shinning'. Why did he address 'the light' in this passage as being 'the True light? It has to be because 'the darkness' referred to was in fact 'false light'. This is what an IOU offers: a brief moment of 'intellectual illumination' – but that is all! This is not conversion and will only lead to further darkness if the addict is not handled with a mixture of gentle strength, prayer and mature Bible study. Light bulb moments never keep anyone clean for any length of time; they are prone to short circuits and power cuts and frequently go out just when you least expect it.

We believe, and therefore teach, that this is what Proverb 3:5-6 is referring to when it says:

"Trust in The Lord with all your heart, and <u>lean not on your own understanding</u>. In all your ways, acknowledge Him and He will guide your path".

Our challenge, at the moment of illumination, is to try and get the clients to acknowledge gratitude to 'the source' of the True Light and to avoid the inclination toward self-edification. If IOU's are not monitored by spiritual eyes, the client will start to relapse even as they appear to be growing.

A true life changing spiritual awakening will always illuminate to the recipient exactly how little they truly understand about life and about right and wrong.

We frequently suggest the following prayer as a guideline toward freedom from the magnetism of self-deception:

"Lord Jesus, I acknowledge how, in the light of your Spirit, my reflections can only really show my dark side and my need of you. I thank you that my depression is a sign of life from you, telling me that something is wrong in me and I agree with how sad my condition is. In sorrow for my sinful state I turn to you".

I acknowledge that the illuminations of understanding that I have received only display your desire to offer me light, and I understand that should my deeds be judged by God, I would stand condemned.

Thank you for what you achieved for me at Calvary when you shed your Blood and died on that Cross to pay the penalty for my sin.

My heart is open before you Lord. Please will you forgive me and fill me with your life giving Holy Spirit.

Guide me now Lord, help me to desire more of you, the True Light, and less of me that I might

Recognize and follow the path of a life that brings you glory, honour and praise"

For years I dragged my life through failure after failure, misery on top of misery, heart-ache on top of heart-ache, and all the time my belief only grew that I was no good. I was just cut out to be one of life's failures. I was born a junky, I'll live a junky and I'll die a junky. Today, I see much much more. Today I see how I was actually in a relationship - which is precisely what I was created for – with the false and temporary influence brought on by the intake of a chemical, from which I thought I was getting the following:

1. Identity Enlightenment
2. Individual Significance
3. Social Security

My dear reader, take a quick look at your life right now and ask yourself: From whom, what or where are you being 'Enlightened'? From whom, what or where are you getting your Individual Significance? From whom, what or where do you get your Security?

Let me offer a check list of suggestions:

- Other people who suffer from a similar addiction to your own as they 'need you'
- Christian ministry
- Acts of charity
- The gym
- The opposite sex
- Your job and the amount you earn
- Your belongings - big house(s), car(s), boats(s)
- Your computer and/or many other electronic idols
- Academic certification

My friend, if you are looking to anything like this for your identity, significance and security, then you too must now start to see how you are fooling (deceiving) yourself. This may explain why your apparent high-life is secretly just as hostile (passive aggressive) and uncomfortable as any addict living the low-life; because the very best of men are men at best and a counterfeit stability can only ever offer a fragile sense of significance.

I personally believe when the day arrives for the curtain of every person's life to be opened before God, there will be just as many hidden agenda's exposed within the 'un-addicted' educated masses as there ever were in the dirtiest of members from the drug culture. It will be at that time, I believe, that many whom the world considered to be guilty will be declared innocent and in stark contrast, many who saw themselves as innocent will be declared guilty.

My dear reader let me ask you; do you really know what it is to be free from that inherent impending sense of doom over your soul? If you had to find yourself sitting in the blistering heat of a hostile wilderness all alone, removed from your every comfort zone, would you then know with a deep and blessed assurance that God's Holy Spirit witnesses to your spirit that you are a child of God? Would there be from within the very depths of your soul the cry of "Abba Father"? Because if not, it may well be that some things in your life may have to be addressed. The first thing being; in all honesty, how much do you really want freedom? How much are you prepared to let go in order to be identified as a child of The Living God? How much damage does that question inflict upon your current belief system? How about relinquishing control of your life to the government of another, and taking ownership of your pride, your lust, your greed, envy, gossiping, jealousy and your selfish ambition? How about sitting in courageous reflection over your condition of desperation without deflection from the gift of depression to establish direction and liberation from your affliction through confession unto salvation in the Christ Jesus, The Son of The Living God?

CHAPTER NINETEEN

CONFESSION

Step 5 "We admitted to ourselves, to God and to another human being the exact nature of our wrongs"

Man's truth looking for God's Grace.

Something has kept the addiction alive and thriving, even fuelled it, almost unto death.

Like an out of control train the addiction ploughs its way through the possessions, the hearts and the minds of every person it comes into contact with. Look at the carnage behind any addict and you will see what looks like the remains of a spiritual hurricane.

Specifics of the nature that fed the addiction have to be nailed. Hopefully now, we have an emerging individual who is starting to see things differently from the days in which he made right sound wrong and wrong sound right. Hopefully we have an emerging individual who is willing to concede that his addiction is not someone else's fault, and the time has come for him to take responsibility for his own life. As we embark on the season of inspirational illuminational reflection, our addict is going to need guidance into the specifics of the nature of his shortcomings. In the addiction treatment industry we have a saying: "we are only as sick as our secrets". In the Church, we pretend everything is alright most of the time, leaders never have any faults and many adopt the position of being like a Royal Family within their congregation. Pastors don't lead by therapeutic discipleship, they sermonize about God's Love.

King David was described by God as "a man after my own heart". I believe that in order to understand what that means, we should look at one of his most famous quotes and follow his example:

Psalm 19:12-14

Who can understand his errors? Oh make me pure from secret faults, and keep your servant back from presumptuous sins; do not let them rule over me; then I shall be upright, and I shall be innocent of great transgression

1. He acknowledged that he had no real understanding of his mistakes

2. He acknowledged that he needed cleaning from his secrecy

3. He acknowledged that he needed help from committing sins of arrogance

4. He acknowledged that his secrets and sins had the power to rule his life

5. He acknowledged that under God's care he could stand with integrity

That's how to become a person after God's own heart - by trusting that God's Grace is only looking for the truth of man.

Concluding Case Studies

Karen sits in my study, a good looking lady who obviously comes from good stock. Karen is highly educated, well spoken and very polite. She professes a Christian belief. Two Christian friends bring Karen to my office because of an ongoing struggle around Cocaine and Alcohol abuse, so we chat about getting real about the reasons for her need for chemical connection and the conversation goes as follows:

Karen: I know the main reasons why I am taking the chemicals and I have confessed them to my pastor, but I am still feeling terribly guilty and ashamed and I cannot stop using.

Me: What have you confessed?

Karen: I slept with my best friend's boyfriend.

Me: Anything else?

Karen: No that's it. I slept with him, felt terrible, confessed it and yet I still feel guilty.

Me: That's because you are still guilty.

Karen: Why? I thought God forgives!

Me: He does, but only when you confess your sins. To own up to sleeping with a friend's boyfriend because you feel guilty, is not confession. Sleeping with the guy was the result of several secret sins.

1. Selfish Ambition
2. Hypocrisy
3. Betrayal
4. Seduction
5. Lust
6. Adultery

Me: Sitting with your Pastor and telling him that you slept with this guy is a summary of your behaviour, probably done as an attempt to appease your own guilt, not because you were truly sorry. The Lord actually says "If you will confess your sins I will forgive you your sins and purify you from all unrighteousness" (1 John 1:9). To confess means nothing less than "agree with the full truth about a specific act", which means we are required to go behind the behaviour and expose the innermost motivations. Once these have been identified and addressed and we resolve in our hearts that this is the truth of our sinfulness, we can then really start to change (repentance). Once we have admitted the truth to ourselves, we can then confess the dynamics involved in the act of 'sleeping with the guy' with another person and to God, who will then faithfully forgive and remove the guilt. God does not purify us from the unrighteousness of greed if we confess sins of envy, but He will purify us from all unrighteousness linked to the sins of which we are truly taking ownership.

Karen: That could take forever!

Me: That's not what the Bible tells us.

Karen: What does it tell us?

Me: The Bible tells that Christians (The Bride of Christ) will eventually reach a place where we will have 'made ourselves ready', but it also tells us that it is The Lord Jesus Christ alone who 'is able to keep us from stumbling' and who will 'present us blameless before the presence of His glory with exceeding joy' (Revelation 19:7 & Jude 24).

Karen (crying): So with my ability even to believe my own lies about why I do things, am I even going to make it to heaven?

Me: That's between you and Him, but it is certainly starting to look like it to me. You are now starting to sound like a woman after God's own heart.

For many months before coming to us, this young lady had actually developed the ability of feeling comfortable with the low-level of honesty she had displayed around her adultery. However, because her personal life remained a shambles, she continued to abuse mind and mood altering chemicals. During my interview with her she became visibly disturbed as we 'penetrated' the truth of what had taken place. We sat and exposed several distortions of her heart until the tears started to flow. Karen went away and felt depressed for several days until she spoke again to her friends and Pastor about the real Karen. Thus far, several years on, Karen has not returned to Cocaine or Alcohol abuse and is enjoying fellowship in her Church.

The confession phase is about identifying the exact nature of our wrongs irrespective of how uncomfortable it may feel. Good Christian therapists learn the art of disturbing the comfortable with the truth of God, so that they can then comfort the disturbed with the love of God. If we do not penetrate the exact nature of the wrong, it stays wrong. Exposure of a fault to someone else does have a therapeutic value, but that is nothing more than a psychological valium. If our damaged and dangerous nature is not exposed and grieved, it will continue to govern the nature of the personality and our choices.

In active destructive addiction I once entered my sister's house and stole money to buy heroin. When she and her husband confronted me I professionally denied everything and turned to the finger of accusation towards her husband so that she apologized to me for accusing me.

This incident played on my mind for months and I continued to feel deeply guilty. When I could not cope with the guilt any longer I went and said 'sorry' because I could not shake off the feelings of guilt. I just wanted the guilt to go away, so I apologized to my sister in order to manipulate her as a means of self-medicating.

Step 5 of the 12 Step recovery programme invites its members to 'admit to God, to ourselves and to another human being the exact nature of our wrongs'. For the final several years of my own addiction I was frequently professing a desire to get clean and remorse over my lifestyle. I entered various treatment facilities trying to get clean and made several attempts at Step 5.

However, what I truly believed to be rigorous honesty in my sharing turned out to be nothing more than a 'verbal acknowledgement to God, to myself and to other human beings a gory summary of my wrongs, with a hidden agenda of either impressing them or winning sympathy from them'.

I never actually admitted in a true confessional sense anything about the exact nature of myself or my motives. I was not able to, because as far as my perception was concerned, it was far too painful to face up to.

I was still deeply ingrained in my self-deceptive mind-set which, in a very cunning way, served my purpose of using heroin again at some point.

Psalm 19:12-14

"Who can understand his errors? Oh make me pure from secret faults, and keep your servant back from presumptuous sins; do not let them rule over me; then I shall be upright, and I shall be innocent of great transgression"

My belief is that each individual from within the ranks of the addicted must be allowed his or her own time to get to a place within themselves where they are truly ready to 'admit to themselves the exact nature of their wrongs'. I also believe that this condition can only really be recognized by a desire for Divine supervision. To venture into the darkest vaults of their deceptive heart unaccompanied can only be a recipe for disappointment and relapse. Therefore there must be a standard of measure in place which can confirm to us that any darkness we might find within ourselves can and will be understood, accepted and forgiven by God in and through The Lord Jesus Christ's sacrifice of Atonement. This way, the back-breaking burdens of addictions can be more than exposed, they can be removed. Many times I have heard people with tears in their eyes declaring 'it is as if a load has been removed from my shoulders' and they, like David, stand upright and innocent of the weight of their transgressions.

The Bible tells us in plain language about the condition of man's heart as far back as Genesis chapter 6:5-6 when we are told that 'God saw that human evil was out of control. People thought evil, imagined evil, evil, evil, evil from morning to night. God was sorry that he had made the human race in the first place; it broke his heart' (The Message).

That's what God sees and that's what broke God's heart. If we refuse to look at ourselves in any depth because we are afraid of what we might see, we can never get to hate what God hates and our hearts may never break over our condition. David was a man after God's own heart, because he faced up to the distortions within him and took ownership of them. Paul the Apostle was also courageous enough to examine himself honestly in depth and came out crying 'Oh what a wretched man I am, who can set me free from this body of death"? Romans 7.

The more you are willing to look at yourself, the more courage you are going to need; the more courage you apply, the more ownership you can take; the more ownership you take, the more you will have to concede that only a miracle can help you. At that point, whoever you are and whatever you have done, you can turn to God in and through The Lord Jesus Christ. You can open your heart and declare your need for forgiveness as you confess your miserable condition and you will receive the truth of God's Fatherly love of you into your heart.

The more you confess, the more you will experience His forgiveness in and through The Lord Jesus Christ. The more you are forgiven, the closer you will continue to get to God as He reconciles you to Himself; and the closer you get to God, the more your life will consist of: Significance, Security and Love - the very things you were looking for in the first place. You will be amazed at how life develops seasoning, reasoning, purpose and direction. At last, because you faced up to your sinful state and agree with God about your need for mercy, you can receive The Lord Jesus as your personal Saviour.

The day can now begin in peace and joy and choice as you start to function in freedom from your previous life-governing destructive desires. The inner-most desires of your heart will start to change and to develop God-ward, as John Piper put it.

The primary desire of your heart will be for people to see God at work in your life and for His name to be recognized. This is something that cannot be achieved by man's effort; this is the miracle of the re-birth.

This spiritual awakening has to take place, where the addict switches from his dying state of bondage into a state of liberation and then, and only then, can a true programme of rehabilitation begin. Up until now, all previously failed and futile visits to rehabilitation centres have been under the governing power of Deception. Now we see that there is actually no such thing as a rehabilitation centre, rehabilitation comes from above and starts within the heart over time, out in the home and in the work place.

Because they are called 'Rehabs', parents and addicts alike, have false hopes and unreasonable expectations. That's why I feel we are seeing more failure than success stories; because of the distorted understandings and expectations. In exactly the same way the addiction was the result of a 'process' - so too must be the goal of 'rehabilitation'.

Let us lower our expectations and allow this new tree to develop through the storms of winter and the droughts of summer before we celebrate. Rehabilitation is the fruit of lengthy clean time in society with freedom of choice through good times and bad. Freedom is not the fruit of rehabilitation - Rehabilitation is the fruit of freedom. `Rehabilitation Programmes in Rehabilitation Centers should therefore, in my opinion, be renamed as 'Liberation Focused Discovery Programmes.

Conclusion = Liberation

We have travelled through The Valley of Addiction and as we now start to ascend the final slopes towards the land flowing with milk and honey, where truth governs, we must remain ever vigilant. We must guard ourselves against the assumption that everything is going to be alright 'from now on'. As was once said, 'a man's worst difficulties begin when he is able to do as he likes' and since The Bible teaches that freedom must always include guidelines and boundaries, the real work of 'growing up' is just about to start.

Early Recovery – the struggle to do the right things for the right reasons – creates a whole new set of problems, some of which feel frightening to the newly liberated individual. At 07:30 on the morning of 22nd December 1993, Her Majesty's Prison Service opened its gates and released me to enter society once again. There were two other guys released with me that day, and I could see myself in them as I used to be on release day and I knew, they were not truly free. They were extremely keen and naturally high on adrenalin because of the 'freedom' just beyond the gate. I found myself feeling a sense of sadness for them. They were very false in their appreciation of each other and full of immature dreams for the immediate future. They had not slept properly for the last two weeks of their sentence, what we called 'Gate Fever', and they believed the whole world would be happy about their release.

Deception still had them, because in truth, at home, worried Moms and girlfriends sat with painted smiles and false hope, actually dreading their return.

Six months before my release, from within the darkest period of my life, The Truth had set me free. I had met with the truth of who Christ Jesus really is during a sermon and within my heart I could only fall at His feet. I caught a glimpse of my sin and I caught a glimpse of His Holiness and I could only plead for mercy. It turned out that Mercy was exactly what He desired to cover me with and at that very moment I went into a personal intimate relationship with God in and through The Lord Jesus. I sought and found forgiveness in and through Jesus Christ, and my soul burst free and I suddenly saw how it was His Blood that covered my sins! I did not stop taking drugs, my addiction was removed. I had not taken any drugs for the closing six months of that sentence and many prisoners came to see and asked how. It was incomprehensible for them and, if I'm honest, it was for me to a degree too. I was clean and at peace, right in the very middle of prison's spiritual and emotional anarchy where I had a variety of reasons to use. However, one thing rested quietly within my heart and mind; I was free, and nothing could threaten the wonderful deep river of peace within me.

So, as the gate opened for me, I was completely calm, chemical free, quietly pre-occupied with one key hope for my future: that I might now be in a position really to grow and to help others find freedom in Christ Jesus to the Glory of God the Father. I now knew that that was the right thing and I knew that was the right reason. What I did not know was, how easy it is to do the right thing, and then claim the glory.

I left the prison six months clean from mind and mood altering chemicals and walking in newness of heart and mind. It came easy for me to concede that life on planet earth in my new state was going to be too much for me to go it alone and I booked myself into a therapeutic home for the treatment of addictions.

Life was good and I knew my drug using days were over. I gratefully adhered to house rules about not going anywhere alone for two weeks and started the struggle to do things correctly. I believed that I was safe enough within myself to go anywhere alone, but that was beside the point; the point was, I now agreed with and applied myself to the rules of life.

On my first trip out of the house alone I went into town and decided to ride the bus. Standing in the bus queue I felt just like everyone else. I did not feel special or different; I did not feel as if everyone knew I was fresh out of jail. I just felt like I belonged here and that I had every right to be here'. It was brand new. I felt an inner sense of joy and elation and everything within me wanted to tell the world that 'I am free, I am free'. When the bus arrived, I was still savoring being a member of the human race right up until it came time for me to pay the driver. As I suddenly found myself face to face with the bus driver, I started to fumble through my pockets for the fare. I only had a five pound note and I was not sure whether or not it would be accepted. My confidence suddenly just fell away from me. I was instantly feeling lost and totally vulnerable. The impatient look on the drivers face hurt me and I was suddenly filled with anxiety. To play for time I asked the driver, "does this bus go to Stroud"? Tapping his steering wheel he sarcastically responded with, "that's what the sign on the front says isn't it"? I lost the plot. I felt this surge of rage erupting from deep within me. Everything within me wanted to grab him by the hair and drag him into the street. I somehow managed to pass him my five pound note, collect my change and make my way to a seat. I sat there trembling with shock and rage. I felt inferior, inadequate and insulted and I felt as if everyone on the bus knew what I was feeling. As those feelings started to subside I slowly started to feel really weepy. I was 34 years of age and did not have the standard social skills or the emotional stability to handle conflict without a knee jerk reaction to resorting to desires for violence. I felt totally alone.

I tried to share this incident with some new Church members with whom I was starting to fellowship. Several of them instantly dismissed my trauma with the wave of a hand and a very negative response of, "Oh bus drivers are all the same". I wasn't complaining about the bus driver; in my own way I was trying to reach out for help with my deepest feelings of vulnerability. I got hurt by the dismissal and once again spontaneously resorted to an old behaviour pattern of silently deciding to keep my mouth shut in future. It was at that point I caught myself attempting to make right sound wrong and wrong sound right by not acknowledging the truth of my hurt and deciding to not practice personal responsibility for my feelings.

Thereafter I took my hurts, failings and insecurities into the local 12 Step Recovery Community of Alcoholics and Narcotics Anonymous where I found unconditional positive regard. I refused to fall back into pretense about how vulnerable I felt out in what I perceived to be a 'big bad world of nasty grown-ups' for any one. I then started to discover what the growth process looked like and I began to trust that as long as my efforts remained faithful and uncompromising around the spiritual principles of truth for the glory of God, the spiritual principles of truth would stand faithful and uncompromising to my efforts and it was then that I started to mature. Only self-seeking could now sabotage my walk with God and my recovery.

I do not in any way want this book to discount the activity of demonic influences in the world today, but I will say I do not believe they have names like 'alcoholism' 'addiction' and 'horny'. It is my firm conviction that these potentially devastating behaviour patterns are firmly rooted in self-seeking. "The devils made me do it" will not in any way vindicate anyone at the judgment seat of God.

Coming out of an addiction means much more than not taking drugs any more. It involves a coming out of beliefs attitudes and behaviours which were in place before the chemicals took over. One of the principle beliefs and behaviours of most addicts before the drug is 'people pleasing'. I personally believe 'people pleasing' to be the first fruits of social anxiety, something all people are supposed to feel, particularly adolescents. Particularly sensitive adolescents feel an exaggerated social anxiety even within their own home and people pleasing is more than a social politeness; it feels like a life saving need. Something within them interprets any form of disapproval as a personal attack and rejection; and these deceiving beliefs turn inward and have the potential to turn toxic and govern a person for their whole life.

Please try to remember that our emmerging individual is only on the brink of joining the Early Recovery process of struggling to do the right things for the right reasons. To them, 'people pleasing' has always been 'the right thing' – it served their need for approval for years. I say this now, because our immerging individual is going to have to start developing internal character – the ability to face problematic circumstances with a solutional mind-set – in the face of what he may once have interpreted as 'failure'. He has never been taught this life skill; it is like trying to learn a new language. However, now, with the help of a safe community of people we start to see that we are actually free to fail from time to time, as long as we are failing forward.

We are free from the government of addiction and its identity-less sub-culture, but even in this new land, we may often feel blind, insecure and incompetent around some of what the world wants us to see as 'normal'.

I personally had to start learning the difference between Safe People and Unsafe People, because all that glistens is not gold. I first had to be de-culturalised from the lifetime of addictive inclinations and re-culturalised into my new life with my new inclinations and my vulnerabilities.

Now I had to start a new process of learning about people's boundaries, because of my history of bringing pain into my relationships.

Now I had to start a new process of learning how to recognize what it is about me that needs to change, instead of focusing on how better off I would be if YOU would just change. Now I had to start a new process of learning about the dynamic of trust, which called for me to get vulnerable about my feelings and failings. Now I had to start a new process of learning to accept the way of life in front me, as opposed to being governed by the way of death behind me. Today, over 16-years clean, I am still frequently failing, but forwards. Today though, people love me, trust me, and in many ways some even admire me, but not everyone, and that's ok.

Jesus once said; "Blessed are you when men shall separate you from their company and cast your name as evil for the sake of The Truth" and "woe to you when all men speak well of you for in the same way their fathers treated the false prophets" (Luke 6:22 & 26 Paraphrased).

To the current and potentially chemically dependent people reading this book, in closing, I leave you with these thoughts; it could be time for you to concede that in and of yourself you can neither define nor compromise God's truth. It could be time for you to accept that you need to come out of hiding and face up to taking personal responsibility for your feelings attitudes and behaviors and it might be time for you to do away with playing the blame game.

To those readers who do not believe that the last statement applies to them, in closing, I leave you with this suggestion; try reading this book again.